ISBN 978-1-629131-07-8

Published by
Remnant Publications, Inc.
649 East Chicago Road
Coldwater, MI 49036

Text written by Bradley Booth
Copyedited by Rudy Hall, Judy Jennings,
Clarissa Fiedler
Edited by Lori Peckham, Jerry Stevens
Cover design by David Berthiaume
Interior design by Eric Pletcher
Cover illustrations by Leandro Tonelli

Portions taken from the original works of E. G. White:
*Patriarchs and Prophets, Prophets and Kings,
The Desire of Ages, The Acts of the Apostles, and
The Great Controversy.*

Printed in China

Way of the Master

Table of Contents

God's Purpose for His Church...4

Preaching With New Power 10

Miracle at the Gate 14

Peter and John in Trouble Again 18

Ananias and Sapphira 24

Peter and John Imprisoned 30

The Stoning of Stephen 34

Philip and the Ethiopian..40

Simon the Sorcerer 44

From Persecutor to Preacher...48

Dorcas Raised to Life...54

Peter and the Sheet 58

Chained Between Two Soldiers..64

Adventures in Antioch 70

An Angry Mob Stones Paul 74

Fighting in Church 80

Timothy Joins Paul 84

Earthquake at Midnight 88

They Turned the World Upside Down! 94

Who Is the Unknown God? 98

Paul at Corinth 104

Healed by a Handkerchief 108

Success and Danger in Ephesus 112

A Young Man Falls to His Death 118

Saved by the Romans 122

Paul Before the Sanhedrin 128

A King Almost Becomes a Christian 132

Shipwrecked! 138

Paul Is Bitten by a Deadly Snake 142

Special Armor for God's Special Forces 146

Paul Helps a Runaway Slave 150

Spreading the Gospel From Prison 154

I Have Fought the Good Fight 158

Peter Is Faithful to the End 164

John Is Boiled in Oil 168

Seven Messages From Seven Churches 172

A Woman and a Child Hunted by a Dragon 178

John Receives a Heavenly Vision 182

God Leads His Church to Success 186

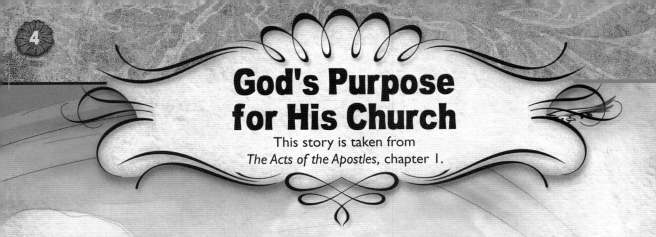

God's Purpose for His Church

This story is taken from
The Acts of the Apostles, chapter 1.

God has always had a group of people in this world who are His chosen ones. They are His children on whom He gives His blessings. They are asked to point the world to Jesus, and sometimes to suffer Satan's persecutions as they spread the good news of the gospel. This group of people God calls His church.

Since the days of Adam and Eve, God has been working through His church to show the world His plan of salvation. Satan deceived earth's first parents, and they lost their garden home. But God wanted to restore them to Eden. As they offered that first lamb sacrifice to God, He pointed them to the day when Jesus would come to die for the sins of the world. As God's people, they were asked to keep the promises of God alive through these offerings.

However, people forgot that plan, and His church became corrupt. Like Cain, they became corrupt in their worship and angry with God for shutting them out of paradise. God loved them, but they became so evil that He finally had to destroy the earth with a flood of waters.

Noah's ark then became God's church to protect His people and save them from destruction. Unfortunately, few accepted that offer, and most died in the waters that covered the earth. Only eight people believed God's warnings and were saved in the ark.

After the flood, God's church had to start over. He was with His church and helped them get a new start, but again Satan was successful in getting people to doubt God's love. Again, His church became corrupt, because people became evil. They did not believe the promise God gave them in the rainbow, that He would never again destroy the world with a flood.

Instead of trusting in God, they built a tower that would tell the world they did not need God's protection. They could take care of themselves. But God mixed up their languages and scattered them across the earth. If He couldn't get them to work together in spreading the gospel so that people would be led back to God and be saved, He would have to get them to work separately. That way, He would keep evil from spreading like a disease.

They still rebelled against His plan. Before long, there was almost no one who worshipped the one true God. Abraham was chosen to begin a great nation that would show the world what God could do with a group of people if they loved Him and would obey His laws. Unfortunately, when the 12 sons of Jacob went to Egypt during the famine, they forgot they were God's church.

Years later when God delivered the children of Israel from Egyptian slavery, He gave them the Ten Commandments on Mount Sinai. They all promised to keep His laws forever. Unfortunately, just 40 days later, they broke their covenant with God and worshipped the golden calf.

But God forgave them. They were His children, and He wanted to live among them. To do this they would need to build

Noah's ark then became God's church to protect His people and save them from destruction.

a sanctuary, which was like a church. In it would be all kinds of things to teach them about His plan for their salvation. There was an altar for burnt offerings, a basin for washing, holy bread, a seven-branched candlestick, an altar of incense, and the ark of the covenant, where God's presence rested on the mercy seat.

When God delivered the children of Israel from Egyptian slavery, He gave them the Ten Commandments on Mount Sinai.

Through the sanctuary, God hoped the surrounding nations would see His love for His people. When they came to Israel, they would see how God had blessed His children. Then they would want to learn about the plan of salvation for themselves.

When God brought His people into the promised land of Canaan, He had great plans for His church. But they didn't drive out their enemies from the territory as God had instructed them to. Because of this, His people became weak spiritually and began to worship idols from the surrounding nations.

This corrupted God's people, and they became as evil as those around them. Then God would allow their enemies to oppress them, and they would pray to Him for help. When a judge such as Gideon or Samuel would help deliver them from their enemies, they would turn again to God, and He would bless them.

Time and again they did this, and when they wanted a king to rule over them, things got worse. Some of the kings were good, such as David and Hezekiah, but many of them were very wicked and did evil. Kings such as Ahab and Manasseh worshipped gods of wood and stone. This broke God's first commandment, which says, "You shall have no other gods before Me." Through the worship of these false gods, they even sacrificed their own children.

God sent prophets such as Elijah, Isaiah, and Jeremiah to tell the people that worshipping these false gods was wrong. They went on to remind His people that they were supposed to be pointing people to the worship of the one true God. Judgments would come if they didn't obey God's voice, but they did not listen. Some prophets they mocked. Some they beat, and some they even killed. Finally, God had to punish His people by sending them into captivity.

But in the pagan lands to which they were taken, God's chosen ones were faithful to witness for their faith. Shadrach, Meshach, and Abed-Nego would not bow to the king's golden idol. Daniel would not stop praying to God. Esther trusted the Lord to save the Jews from a death decree.

Again, God had mercy on His people. After 70 years of captivity in Babylon, He brought them back to Jerusalem and helped them rebuild the temple and city walls. Unfortunately, they forgot their covenant with God and failed to live for Him. They didn't bring tithes and offerings to the temple. They didn't keep the Sabbath, and they were corrupt in their courts of law.

Men such as Ezra and Nehemiah helped bring God's church back to God, and again the people made a covenant or promise with Him. However, as the years passed they forgot about the promises they had made to God. By the time Jesus was born, most of the Jewish leaders preferred the traditions of men to the commandments of God.

Jesus had come to show His people a better way. He had traveled everywhere healing people of their diseases and preaching the good news of the gospel. He pointed people to the love of the Father and showed them that salvation was for the poor as well as the rich. For these reasons, almost everyone loved Jesus and said that He must be the Messiah, except for the chief priests and scribes, who saw Him as the enemy. Although they were impressed that He was the Messiah and the Son of God, they crucified Him on a cross.

When Jesus died for the sins of the world, it changed everything. The old ways had passed away, and everything that had pointed to Jesus as the Lamb of God was fulfilled. The purpose for God's church didn't change, only the way we did things.

When Jesus died for the sins of the world, it changed everything. The old ways had passed away.

Now God would ask His people once again to take the gospel to the world. God's church rose up to proclaim the good news that Jesus is a risen Savior. His people would spread the message that Jesus is coming soon as King of kings and Lord of lords to take His people home.

God's people are His church. This means that if you and I claim to believe in Jesus and want to spend forever with Him, we are His church. The choice we have is the same as all of those we read about. We will either take the message of a risen Savior to the world or decide that our own wants are more important, and we will be led away by Satan. Make the right choice today!

Hidden Treasure Questions:

✔ Who were the first two members of God's church on earth?

✔ Name five people in the Old Testament who stood as witnesses for God.

Listen to this story online!

Scan for bonus content

Preaching With New Power

This story is taken from Acts 2 and
The Acts of the Apostles, chapter 4.

The Day of Pentecost had come! The disciples had gathered in the upper room to put aside their differences and pray. Now God had poured out His Holy Spirit on them. A mighty rushing wind had filled the room, and flames of fire had hovered above every believer in the room. It was clear that God had come to give them something they had never had before.

Now armed with the power of God, they were about to do great things for Him. Jesus had told them that He would come again, but first they must share the gospel with the world! This must have been a very exciting thought and a little scary, too.

Their first assignment was to go to the temple. The power of the Holy Spirit had come upon them, and now they felt that it was time to share the good news of Jesus' resurrection.

So off they went singing and praising God, with more excitement than they had ever had before. The change that had come over them was amazing. Before they had received the Holy Spirit, they had been afraid to speak as witnesses for Jesus. They were afraid that the Jewish priests and elders might come and do the same things to them that they had done to Jesus.

When they arrived at the temple, the place was packed. After all, it was the Feast of Pentecost, and thousands of worshippers had come from everywhere to celebrate the religious holiday. Parthians and Medes, Elamites and Arabs were there. Travelers from Mesopotamia, Cappadocia, Pontus, Asia, Egypt, Libya, and Rome came by the hundreds and thousands.

The disciples had seen crowds such as this before, because they had been worshipping at Jewish feast days such as Pentecost their whole lives. But this time it was different. Now they felt the urge to speak for God and tell these visitors about the sad events that had happened in Jerusalem recently.

All of the disciples stood up in the temple and began to share the good news of the gospel. They were so excited. As they began to talk, it became obvious that they were all speaking in the different languages of the people gathered in the temple courtyard. The crowds listened in amazement! It was wonderful! We can imagine how excited they must have been to have someone teaching the gospel to them in their own language, whether it was Egyptian, Libyan, Arabic, or Latin.

It was all quite amazing! Before long those from Egypt probably gathered around the disciple who was speaking Egyptian. Those from Libya would have listened to the disciple speaking Libyan. The Arabians would have stood around the disciple speaking Arabic.

There were many who did not see the

God had poured out His Holy Spirit. A mighty rushing wind had filled the room, and flames of fire had hovered above every believer.

importance of the day. Instead, they made fun of the disciples. They had never seen anything such as this in their entire lives, and they probably didn't know what to think. Were the disciples crazy? Had they drunk too much wine?

Peter seems to have been the main speaker for the day. "Listen, everyone," he said, "we are all quite normal and not drunk as you might think. What you see here today is the power of God at work so that everyone can hear the good news of the gospel in their own language. It is a miracle, indeed! As the prophet Joel said, 'In the last days God will pour out His Spirit on our sons and daughters, on servants and masters, and on old and young alike.'

"The biggest news of all," said Peter, "is that Jesus of Nazareth, God's Son, lived among us for years, doing miracles and performing signs and wonders. Unfortunately, not everyone liked Him. Tragically, the Jewish leaders unjustly accused Him. He suffered, bled, and died when He was nailed to a wooden cross. He gave His life for the sins of the world.

"But that wasn't the end of the story! God raised Jesus from the dead, and then took Him to heaven, where He is now standing at the right hand of God."

"Repent and be baptized, every one, of you in the name of Jesus."

No one spoke at first, but then someone in the crowd must have broken the silence. "What shall we do?" he asked. "We are guilty as you have said," and then everyone joined him, because they now felt the power of God calling them to repentance.

"Repent and be baptized, every one of you, in the name of Jesus so your sins can be washed away!" Peter replied. "Then you can receive the gift of the Holy Spirit."

God blessed the believers that day in Jerusalem. Many came forward to give their hearts to Jesus and to be baptized. In fact, 3,000 believers were added to the church that day. What a blessing that must have been! Surely the angels of God must have sung in celebration for all that God had done for the brand-new church!

Our Prayer:

"Dear God, please prepare my heart so that I can serve You wherever I go. Let me speak for You in any language that can help others and bring glory to God."

Hidden Treasure Questions:

✔ How many people were baptized on the Day of Pentecost in Jerusalem?

✔ Do you think it is possible that God could someday ask you to share the gospel story for Him in another language?

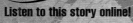
Listen to this story online!

Scan for bonus content

Miracle at the Gate

This story is taken from Acts 3 and
The Acts of the Apostles, chapter 6.

The outpouring of the Holy Spirit on the disciples in the upper room was an amazing event. No one had ever seen anything like it in Jerusalem, and the power of God was being demonstrated in many miraculous ways. To the temple crowds on the Day of Pentecost the disciples had preached in languages that they didn't even speak. Every day that passed now brought new signs and wonders for people to witness.

A few days after Pentecost, John and Peter were on their way up to the temple to worship when they saw a crippled man sitting at the Beautiful Gate. The lame man had lived a life of pain and suffering for 40 years, since the day of his birth.

For a long time, he had wanted to see Jesus so that he might be healed. Unfortunately, there was no one to help him, so he couldn't get to the places where Jesus preached and healed.

Finally, he got some friends to carry him to the temple gate, where he looked for Jesus. However, when he arrived he discovered that the One who could have healed him had been crucified.

He was so discouraged that he didn't know what to do, so he continued his life of begging. "Alms for a poor man!" he called to the people going into the temple.

Peter and John had been fishermen all their lives and had been followers of Jesus for more than three years. They were very poor themselves, but they couldn't go by the lame man without saying something kind to him.

The Holy Spirit then inspired Peter to give the poor man more than just a greeting. "Silver and gold I do not have, but what I do have I give you," Peter said. "In the name of Jesus Christ of Nazareth, rise up and walk."

To the man's surprise, Peter took his hand and lifted him up, and suddenly he could walk. His feet and ankle bones received strength, and immediately he began jumping and praising God. As Peter and John went on up into the temple, the man who had been crippled followed them, shouting his thanks to God for this miraculous healing.

Everyone in the temple heard the shouting and came running to see what all the commotion was about. When they saw the man walking and praising God, they were amazed. They knew this man as the cripple who had been sitting begging for alms at the Beautiful Gate, and now he was walking!

The man was so excited! As Peter and John entered Solomon's Porch, he clung to them as if he was afraid to let them go. By now, hundreds of worshippers were crowding around to hear his story.

Peter looked around at all the people in surprise. "Men of Israel, why do you marvel at this?" he asked. "Why look so intently at us, as though by our own power or godliness we have made this man walk? The God of our fathers Abraham, Isaac, and Jacob glorified His Servant Jesus, whom you delivered up and denied in the presence of

Peter said, "In the name of Jesus Christ of Nazareth, rise up and walk."

Pilate, when he wanted to let Him go. But you denied the Holy One and asked for a murderer to be granted to you, and killed the Prince of life whom God raised from the dead, of which we are witnesses. Faith in the name of Jesus has made this man strong, whom you see and know. Yes, the faith that comes through Jesus Christ has healed this man in the presence of you all.

"Yet now I know that you did this in ignorance just as the rulers did. But those things that God foretold by the mouth of all His prophets, that the Christ would suffer, He has fulfilled. Repent therefore and be converted, that your sins may be blotted out, so that times of refreshing may come from the presence of the Lord."

To the man's surprise, Peter took his hand and lifted him up, and suddenly he could walk.

This kind of preaching was sure to get Peter and John into trouble, and sure enough it did. When the priests and Sadducees heard that the disciples were talking about Jesus' resurrection from the dead again, it made them really angry. They had killed Jesus and hoped that everyone would forget about Him.

But the memory of Jesus' life and death wasn't going away. In fact, the stories of His resurrection were spreading everywhere now, and the disciples wouldn't stop preaching about it. The numbers of Christians were growing so fast that no one knew for sure how many there were. Some said as many as 5,000.

Our Prayer:

"Dear Heavenly Father, I want to be as brave as Peter and John and be a witness for You."

Hidden Treasure Questions:

✔ Which gate in the temple was the crippled man sitting at when Peter and John healed him?

✔ Who was really angry when they heard that Peter and John were preaching about Jesus' resurrection?

Listen to this story online!

Scan for bonus content

Peter and John in Trouble Again

This story is taken from Acts 4 and
The Acts of the Apostles, chapter 6.

Everyone was excited when they heard about Peter and John healing the crippled man at the temple gate, but Peter told them they should not be surprised. The man had been healed through the power of Jesus, whom the chief priests and elders had killed.

This made the priests and Sadducees very angry. "Arrest those men!" they ordered, and since it was already evening, the temple guards locked them up until the next day.

It was becoming more obvious every day now that the name of Jesus was more popular than any person at the temple, even the high priest. The Sadducees were desperate to stop this message of Jesus' resurrection from spreading any further. They did not believe in resurrections of any kind, now, or in the future. If this Christian message wasn't stopped, the religion of the Sadducees would die out.

The Pharisees hated the Christians too. They didn't like them because the Christian religion cared less about the Jewish ceremonies than it did about preaching that Jesus had died for the sins of the world.

"Arrest those men!" they ordered, and since it was already evening, the temple guards locked them up until the next day.

The next morning the Jewish leaders sent for the disciples so they could question them about the healing of the crippled man. Many of the scribes and elders were there, and so was the high priest, Caiaphas, and all his family members.

"By what power or by what name have you done this?" the high priest demanded of Peter and John as the trial began.

Peter stepped forward, and he was suddenly filled with the Holy Spirit. "Rulers of the people and elders of Israel," he said, "this day we are being judged for a

good deed done to a helpless man, and by what means he has been made well. Therefore, let it be known to you all, and to all the people of Israel, that by the name of Jesus Christ of Nazareth whom you crucified, whom God raised from the dead, this man stands here before you whole. Jesus is the stone that was rejected by you builders, which has become the chief cornerstone of His church. Nor is there salvation in any other, for there is no other name under heaven given among men by which we must be saved."

All the priests and elders were amazed at the boldness of these disciples! Peter and John were uneducated and untrained, and yet they spoke eloquently, just as Jesus had done. It was obvious that they had been with Him.

Meanwhile, the cripple who had been healed was standing there watching the trial. The priests knew there was nothing

"Let's threaten the disciples, and tell them that they can no longer speak to anyone about this Jesus."

they could do about the miracle. It had obviously happened and was drawing a lot of attention from the crowds. But it was the preaching about Jesus and His resurrection that the priests felt they had to do something about. If they let the disciples go on talking about it, all of Jerusalem would be turning to Christianity to join the church. Then they wouldn't come to the priests at the temple anymore to be taught the way of salvation.

The temple leaders sent the disciples out of the room so that they could talk among themselves. "What shall we do to these men?" they asked one another. "The miracle has been done through them and is now known by everyone in Jerusalem. We cannot deny it. However, neither can we allow the news of this man's healing to spread any further among the people in Jerusalem and all Judea. Let's threaten the disciples, and tell them that they can no longer speak to anyone about this Jesus."

So that is what they did. However, Peter and John were not scared. "Whether it is right in the sight of God to listen to you more than to God, you be the judge," they said. "We are only telling people about the things that we have seen and heard."

After one more round of threats from the priests and Sadducees, they finally let the disciples go. There was no way to punish them, because all the people had seen the miracle and were praising God for it.

When Peter and John left the council, they immediately went to find the other believers to tell them everything that had happened. When the believers had heard the story of their witness for Jesus, they all praised God together.

"Lord, You are God, who made heaven and earth and the sea and all that is in them," they prayed. "You know all things and are in control of all things. In vain did the Jewish leaders persecute You and kill You because it was Your plan all along to die for the human race. Now, Lord, listen to the threats of the Jewish leaders, and help us that we may speak with boldness and do signs and wonders through the name of Your holy Servant Jesus."

When they had finished praying, the room where they were gathered together was shaken, and they were once again filled with the Holy Spirit. Then they went out to speak the Word of God boldly and to do many more signs and wonders among the people.

People brought the sick out into the streets and laid them on beds and couches, in hopes that at least the shadow of disciples such as Peter passing by might fall on some of them. It was all so amazing! God's work was moving forward because of all the preaching and miracles the disciples were doing.

The crowds were now coming from the surrounding cities near Jerusalem, too. They were bringing sick people and those who were tormented by unclean spirits so that they might all be healed. Jesus had healed many people when He was on earth. He had told the disciples that they would do even greater things than He had done.

The priests and Sadducees finally let the disciples go. There was no way to punish them, because all the people had seen the miracle.

Many Jews in Jerusalem admired the followers of Jesus for all they were doing to glorify God, but they dared not join them. They were too afraid of the Jewish priests and elders. Nevertheless, the number of believers in the church continued to increase rapidly. Every day multitudes were joining the Christians in Jerusalem, both men and women, and even many priests were coming forward for baptism.

God was doing mighty things in Jerusalem, just as He said He would. There was no denying that God was blessing the new church.

Dear Jesus, I want to have courage just as Peter and John did. Give me the chance to speak for You as they did."

Hidden Treasure Questions:

✓ Why did the priests and Sadducees want to put Peter and John in prison?

✓ What happened when Peter's shadow fell on the sick people in the streets?

Listen to this story online!

Scan for bonus content

Ananias and Sapphira

This story is taken from Acts 4 and 5 and
The Acts of the Apostles, chapter 7.

The church was growing by leaps and bounds now, and everyone was so excited. Jesus had given His followers power to preach and heal in His name and was helping them spread the good news of the gospel everywhere. Jesus had told the disciples that when the gospel was preached in the whole world, He would come again.

With great power, the apostles told the story of Jesus' death and resurrection. And God's grace was upon them all. Their mission to take the gospel to the world made everyone feel as if they were one big family. Those who believed were of one heart and one soul, and it also made them want to share what they had. There was so much love and care among the believers by now that everyone was giving whatever they could to the church.

Ananias decided he would keep back part of the money, but then lie and say that he was giving all of it.

No one seemed to lack for anything among the early Christians. Many who owned land or houses sold them and brought the money to lay at the apostles' feet. This is how the church raised money to help those in need.

For example, there was a believer from Cyprus named Barnabas who had land and sold it. The land brought a good price, and he donated it for the work of the church in Jerusalem.

Also, there was a man named Ananias and his wife, Sapphira, who also had land and sold it at this time. They had promised that whatever money they got for selling the land would be donated to the church.

However, after the land was sold, they began to wish they had not promised to give all the money. Would it be all right to reconsider their decision? they asked each other.

Unfortunately, Ananias and Sapphira were both very proud. They knew that giving so much money could bring them prestige and popularity in the church, and they wanted that. Others such as Barnabas had been highly praised after giving his large gift.

Ananias decided he would keep back part of the money, but then lie and say that he was giving all of it. His wife also was part of that decision. In this way, they could receive the praise they wanted so much and be able to eat the food that was provided to everyone at the church. Besides all this, they would secretly get to keep part of the money for themselves.

However, when Ananias brought the money to lay at the apostles' feet, things did not go the way he had expected at all. The Holy Spirit showed

When Ananias heard Peter say those things, he fell down on the floor and died.

Peter the truth about how much money Ananias had really sold the land for.

Ananias lied to Peter, saying, "We sold the land for such and such."

But Peter was not happy and said, "Ananias, why has Satan filled your heart to lie to the Holy Spirit and keep back part of the price of the land for yourself? While it remained yours, was it not your own? After it was sold, was it not still in your own control? Why have you conceived this thing in your heart? You have not lied to men, but to God."

It must have been a real shock for Ananias to hear such words. Only he and his wife, Sapphira, knew the details about the sale.

Then a most astonishing thing happened! When Ananias heard Peter say those things, he fell down on the floor and died. Everyone in the room must have been stunned, because no one had ever seen anything like it. Immediately, the young men in the church wrapped Ananias up, carried him out to a cemetery, and buried him.

Word spread quickly, and everyone got real serious as the story was told and retold. That someone had lied to God and died for it was a very solemn thought. It showed them all what God thought of lying.

About three hours later, Sapphira came to the meeting place. Maybe she was coming to eat with the others, or maybe she was looking for her husband. She knew nothing about what had happened to Ananias. However, when Peter asked her if she and her husband had sold the land for so much, she said, "Yes, we sold the land for such and such."

Peter couldn't believe his ears. "How is it that you and your husband have agreed together to test the Spirit of the Lord?" he rebuked her through the power of the Holy Spirit. "Look, the feet of those who have buried your husband are at the door, and they will carry you out, too."

Then she fell down and died right there in front of everyone just as her husband had. The young men who had buried her husband carried her out, too, and buried her beside him.

This story spread far and wide in Jerusalem and to Judea beyond. As a result, everyone had great respect for the apostles, and the young church and the gospel went everywhere as fast as wildfire.

There are valuable lessons to learn from this story. Sin began with Satan, and he is the father of lies. Anyone who does not live to bring honor and glory to God for His wonderful gift of eternal life is living for self and the evil one. Many spend money extravagantly on themselves. They are careless with the blessings of time, talents, and treasure that God has given them.

But God has no place in His church for such people. They may fool themselves into believing that they are serving God because they attend church regularly and give of their money from time to time. But they are serving God only when it is convenient, and when it will make them look good. As Ananias and Sapphira did, they promise such and such for the work of God, but when it is to their advantage, they change their minds or even forget that they made promises at all.

God does not forget His promises to us. He loves us, and He will never lie to us. Jesus is very disappointed when we lie to Him. If we make a promise to someone, we should keep our word. How much more important should it be to keep our promises to God? Moses said, "Be sure your sin will find you out" (Numbers 32:23). You may hide your sins from others for a while, but God always knows everything you do.

You may hide your sins from others for a while, but God always knows everything you do.

God wants us to always be truthful and honest, not only to please Him but for ourselves. Jesus said, "I have come that they may have life, and that they may have it more abundantly" (John 10:10). That simply means that Jesus wants us not only to have life, but to have a healthy, happy life.

If you lie to your parents or to anyone else, you will not be happy very long. If you tell a lie, then confess it and make it right. If you ask God to help you to always be honest, He will. Then you will be a delight to God, your parents, and your friends.

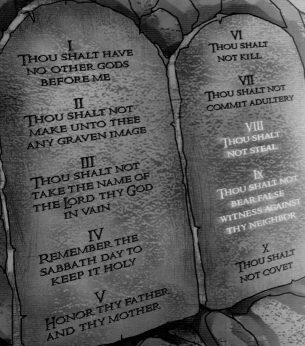

I
THOU SHALT HAVE NO OTHER GODS BEFORE ME

II
THOU SHALT NOT MAKE UNTO THEE ANY GRAVEN IMAGE

III
THOU SHALT NOT TAKE THE NAME OF THE LORD THY GOD IN VAIN

IV
REMEMBER THE SABBATH DAY TO KEEP IT HOLY

V
HONOR THY FATHER AND THY MOTHER

VI
THOU SHALT NOT KILL

VII
THOU SHALT NOT COMMIT ADULTERY

VIII
THOU SHALT NOT STEAL

IX
THOU SHALT NOT BEAR FALSE WITNESS AGAINST THY NEIGHBOR

X
THOU SHALT NOT COVET

Our Prayer:

"Dear God, help me to remember that when I don't tell the truth, I am lying to You."

Hidden Treasure Questions:

✔ What were the names of the man and his wife who promised to give money to the church?

✔ What did the couple tell Peter that made them both die?

Listen to this story online!

Scan for bonus content

Peter and John Imprisoned

This story is taken from Acts 5 and
The Acts of the Apostles, chapter 8.

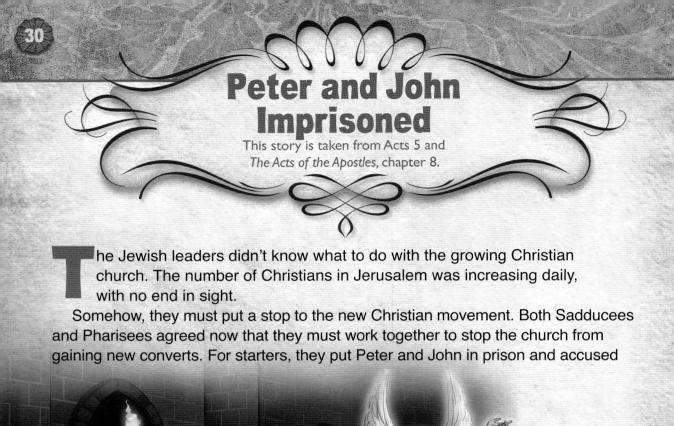

The Jewish leaders didn't know what to do with the growing Christian church. The number of Christians in Jerusalem was increasing daily, with no end in sight.

Somehow, they must put a stop to the new Christian movement. Both Sadducees and Pharisees agreed now that they must work together to stop the church from gaining new converts. For starters, they put Peter and John in prison and accused

them of murdering Ananias and Sapphira. If they could make the crowds angry enough over such an accusation, maybe a mob would beat the disciples to death.

However, that night an angel of the Lord opened the prison doors and brought them out. "Go stand in the temple and speak to the people all the words of eternal life," said the angel.

And, of course, the two disciples obeyed. Early the next morning at daybreak, they went to the temple and began teaching and preaching, as usual.

When the high priest and the other Sadducees came to the temple that morning, they called all the members of the Jewish council together for a trial. Then they sent for Peter and John, who were supposed to be in prison.

However, the temple officers who had been sent to the prison came back with a report that the disciples were not there. They said, "Indeed, we found the prison shut securely and the guards standing outside the doors, but when we opened them, we found no one inside!"

The high priest didn't know what to say, nor did the captain of the temple guards, nor the chief priests. What had happened to the disciples? they wondered. Where had they gone?

Then someone came to the council of elders and said, "The men whom you put in prison are standing in the temple and teaching the people!"

The captain of the temple guard went with the officers to bring Peter and John back with them quietly. The Jewish leaders were afraid to use violence. They knew the crowds might stone them if they did anything to harm the disciples of Jesus, because the common people admired them so much.

> That night an angel of the Lord opened the prison doors and brought them out. "Go stand in the temple and speak to the people all the words of eternal life," said the angel.

When Peter and John were finally brought before the council, the high priest was very angry with them. "Didn't we command you not to teach in Jesus' name?" he demanded. "Now look, you have filled Jerusalem with your doctrine and intend to bring this Man's blood on us!"

Peter and John answered, "We ought to obey God rather than men. The God of our fathers raised up Jesus, whom you murdered by hanging on a tree. God has exalted Him to His right hand to be Prince and Savior, to give repentance to Israel, and forgiveness of sins. And we are His witnesses to these things, and so also is the Holy Spirit, whom God has given to those who obey Him."

When the Jewish council heard this, they were furious and began planning how they could kill the disciples. They didn't care that it was against the law. Only the Romans could carry out executions, but the chief priests were so angry that they were capable of doing anything at the moment.

However, there was one man among them who recognized the voice of God in what the disciples were saying. He was a Pharisee named Gamaliel, a teacher of the law, and everyone in the council respected him.

After they sent the disciples outside, he spoke to the council in words that they would never forget: "Men of Israel, take heed to yourselves what you intend to do regarding these men. Keep away from these men and let them alone, for if this plan or this work is of men, it will come to nothing. However, if it is of God, you cannot overthrow it, lest you be found to fight against God."

Peter and John answered, "We ought to obey God rather than men."

The council agreed and brought the disciples back in. They were severely beaten, and then told that they must not speak in the name of Jesus anymore.

When the disciples were finally allowed to leave, they praised God that they were counted worthy to suffer shame for Jesus.

What a testimony for all of us! What a lesson in humble devotion for Jesus! It didn't matter that Peter and John had just been whipped for preaching in Jesus' name. Nothing could stop them from telling people about Jesus.

Our Prayer:

"Dear Jesus, help me to be a brave witness for You, no matter what the cost."

Hidden Treasure Questions:

✓ Why did the priests arrest Peter and John?

✓ What did Gamaliel say to keep the priests from killing Peter and John?

Listen to this story online!

Scan for bonus content

The Stoning of Stephen

This story is taken from Acts 6 and 7 and
The Acts of the Apostles, chapter 10.

The early church was growing so fast that no one really knew how many Christians there were. Besides this, large numbers of priests were now accepting the message of Jesus' death and resurrection. This was a wonderful blessing. By now, so many people in Judea were filled with the Holy Spirit that the gospel was going everywhere. However, there was a growing problem that needed to be taken care of and soon. Many poor people and widows had joined the church, and they had no one who could look after them. The apostles knew that these people needed food and clothes, but the task

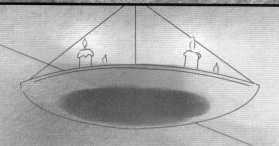
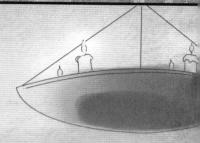

of preparing food and serving it was beginning to take too much of their time. As a result, they were spending less and less time preaching the Word of God.

So the apostles came up with a really great idea. Why not choose seven men and appoint them as deacons in the church so that they could help lighten the apostles' workload? They chose Philip, Prochorus, Nicanor, Timon, Parmenas, Nicolas, and Stephen for service.

Stephen was a man especially filled with the Holy Spirit and full of faith and power. He did many miracles and signs among the people of Jerusalem and was a wonderful preacher.

The apostles came up with a really great idea. Why not choose seven men and appoint them as deacons?

However, trouble was on the way for him. Satan was not happy about all that Stephen was doing to point people to Jesus, and he now stirred up the priests and elders against him. Instead of admitting that Stephen spoke the truth when he preached about Jesus' resurrection, the Jewish leaders hardened their hearts and hated him even more.

There was a special group of Jews in Jerusalem who decided that they would try Stephen as a criminal against the nation. They liked to debate spiritual things, but when they talked with Stephen and tried to draw him into an argument, he had an answer from the Bible for everything they said.

That made this Jewish group angry, and they began plotting how they could bring Stephen to trial to kill him. Part of the plan was for the priests, temple elders, and scribes to start a rumor in Jerusalem that Stephen was a troublemaker. They accused him of criticizing Moses and God in a public meeting. Then they all formed a mob and went in search of him.

When they found him, they grabbed him and brought him to the Jewish council. Saul of Tarsus, a brilliant young Pharisee, was in charge of the trial. He spoke eloquently and with such logic that everyone thought the trial would end quickly.

Stephen gave the people in the Jewish council a Bible study that included some Jewish history.

However, Saul could see that Stephen knew the Scriptures well and knew exactly why he was preaching the news of Jesus' death and resurrection.

Then two false witnesses gave testimony against Stephen in the Jewish court. "We have heard him speak blasphemous words against Moses, the temple, and God," the witnesses said. This stirred up everybody in the court. "We have heard him say that Jesus of Nazareth will destroy this place and change the customs that Moses delivered to us," they added.

The crowd that had gathered in the Sanhedrin was getting angrier every minute, but when they looked at Stephen, his face was glowing like the face of an angel.

The high priest was frightened when he saw this, but he knew that they couldn't let Stephen get away. "Are these things so?" he finally asked, giving Stephen a chance to answer the charges.

Stephen did not give a short answer to the accusations they were bringing on him. Instead, he gave the people in the Jewish council a Bible study that included some Jewish history. As he spoke, his voice was clear and strong, and his eloquence held the audience spellbound.

He began with the story of how God had led Abraham out of Mesopotamia to live in Canaan. Abraham had no place to call his own then, and he had no children. However, God made a covenant with him and promised that he would have as many descendants as there were stars in the night sky.

Stephen also told the story of Joseph being sold into Egyptian slavery by his brothers. He reminded the council that Joseph was faithful to God even in hard times. God knew that He could trust Joseph and blessed him by making him the second-highest ruler in Egypt next to Pharaoh. When there was a terrible famine, Joseph was ready for it. He had prepared for the famine, because God had shown him that the famine was coming.

Finally, Stephen shared the story of Moses. He was born an Israelite baby at a time when the new pharaoh knew nothing about Joseph and what he had done to save Egypt. Because there was a decree to kill all the baby boys, Moses' mother hid him in a basket in the river to save his life. But Pharaoh's daughter rescued him and adopted him as her own.

When he was 40, he tried to deliver the Israelites his own way by killing an Egyptian slave master. Then he had to flee Egypt and went to live in Midian. Finally, God appeared to him in a burning bush and told him that he needed to return to Egypt to deliver the Israelites from slavery. "Let My people go," Moses told Pharaoh when he arrived in Egypt, but the Egyptian ruler didn't listen.

Moses became great in the eyes of all Israel when God punished the Egyptians for not obeying Him. However, even after God sent 10 plagues upon the land of Egypt and parted the Red Sea to deliver them, many Israelites still doubted

His goodness. That is why God punished them by making them wander in the wilderness for 40 years.

"And you people are no different today," said Stephen. "Just like your forefathers, you are stiff-necked and always resist the Holy Spirit! Your fathers persecuted all the prophets! They even killed the ones who prophesied about the coming of Jesus, whom you betrayed and murdered."

> **Stephen knew his last hour had come, and he prayed, "Lord Jesus, receive my spirit!"**

Up until now the members of the Jewish council had been listening politely, but now their eyes once again blazed with anger and hate.

But Stephen was filled with the Holy Spirit, and he had a vision right there in the Sanhedrin. "Look! I see the heavens opened and the Son of Man standing at the right hand of God!" he said.

This infuriated the crowd in the Sanhedrin even more. They covered their ears and jumped up to grab him. Then they dragged him out of the city to stone him, and Saul, the young lawyer who had presented the case in court, was there to give his blessing.

Stephen knew his last hour had come, and he prayed, "Lord Jesus, receive my spirit!" As he knelt there with the stones hitting him, he cried, "Lord, do not charge them with this sin." Then he fell asleep in Jesus.

Our Prayer:

"Dear Jesus, if I should ever have to give my life for You, I pray that I will be as brave as Stephen."

Hidden Treasure Questions:

✔ Why did the Jews hate Stephen so much?

✔ How do we know that Stephen forgave those who were stoning him?

Listen to this story online!

Scan for bonus content

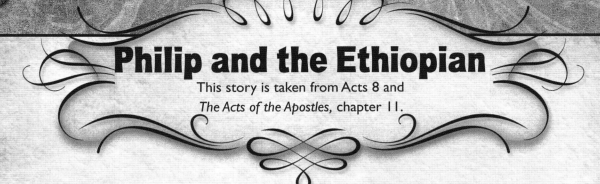

Philip and the Ethiopian

This story is taken from Acts 8 and
The Acts of the Apostles, chapter 11.

Philip loved Jesus so much that he was willing to go anywhere to spread the gospel. It wasn't safe in Jerusalem anymore because Saul of Tarsus was persecuting the Christians there. So Philip left, just like many of the other Christians who were fleeing to cities far and wide. He would have to go somewhere else to preach the gospel story.

One place Philip went was Samaria. Everyone there loved him because of all the wonderful things he did. Besides telling everyone that Jesus was the Messiah, he performed many miracles of healing. He cast demons out of sick people. He healed the lame and those who were paralyzed. There was great joy in Samaria because of Philip.

One day an angel came to visit Philip, saying "Go south on the desert road that runs from Jerusalem to Gaza."

Philip was in the habit of obeying the voice of God.

So he began the journey down the hot, dusty road to Gaza. While on the road he must have prayed, "Show me the next person to whom I need to tell the story of salvation."

As he was walking along the road, he saw a very important-looking man sitting in a chariot reading from a scroll. The voice of God spoke to Philip, telling him to catch up with the chariot and walk along beside it. That was just the kind of invitation Philip needed, and off he went.

When he caught up with the chariot, he noticed that the man was reading a Hebrew scroll of the Scriptures.

"I see you are reading from the book of Isaiah," Philip said. "Do you understand what you are reading?"

"I'd like to, but it's difficult," the officer said. "If I had someone to explain it to me, it would be better."

Can't you just see Philip smiling at that moment? The angel had told him to come down this road, and now he knew why. This man wanted to understand the Scriptures.

"With the help of God I can explain the passage to you," Philip said.

So the officer invited Philip to come and sit with him in the chariot to read the scroll with him as they traveled along.

The man was from Africa and worked in the royal treasury for Candace, the Queen of Ethiopia. He had a lot of influence in his important position and could share what he learned. He believed in God and was on his way home from worshipping in Jerusalem.

The Ethiopian read in his scroll, "He was led as a lamb to the slaughter, and as a sheep before its shearer is silent, so He opened not His mouth. He was taken from prison and from judgment, and who will declare His generation? For He was cut off from the land of the living."

The angel told Philip, "Go south on the desert road that runs from Jerusalem to Gaza."

"Now tell me, please," the Ethiopian asked, "who is the prophet talking about? Is it himself or someone else?"

So Philip began to explain the prophecy found in Isaiah 53. "Jesus of Nazareth is that Lamb," he said. "He was sent from heaven as God the Son to save the world. He was born as a baby, grew to manhood, and preached the good news of salvation. He healed the sick and brought hope to our world. But wicked men killed Him and He did not resist, and so you see how He was brought as a lamb to the slaughter. This Jesus, whom I am telling you about, was resurrected from the dead, ascended to heaven, and now stands in the presence of God our Father."

The Ethiopian kept nodding his head as Philip talked, and it was clear that he now understood and accepted what he was learning. So Philip continued telling him about Jesus' life and explaining how He had fulfilled all the prophecies in the Bible about the Messiah.

"I believe that what you have told me is the truth," the Ethiopian said with a smile. They traveled along a few more miles as they talked, until they passed a flowing stream. "Look, here is water," said the Ethiopian. "What should keep me from being baptized today?"

"If you truly believe with all your heart, you may," Philip said.

"I believe that Jesus Christ is the Son of God." So he stopped his chariot, and Philip and the Ethiopian officer went down into the water, and Philip baptized him.

We can just imagine how happy that man must have been after hearing the story of salvation! Jesus loved him and had come to this earth and died for his sins. Now He was in heaven preparing a home for the Ethiopian and would come someday soon to take all of God's people to heaven. Could there possibly be any better news anywhere in the world?

Then something else happened at that moment. The Bible says that "when they came up out of the water, the Spirit of the Lord caught Philip away." The Ethiopian didn't see him again, but went on his way singing and praising God.

"Look, here is water," said the Ethiopian. "What should keep me from being baptized today?"

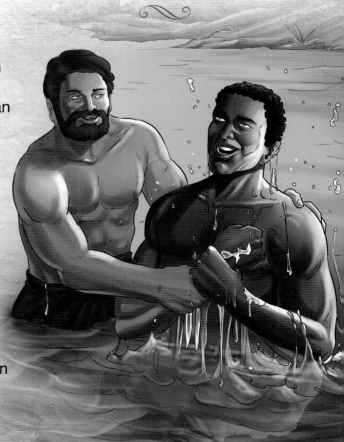

Dear Jesus, please help me to know my Bible better so I can tell others about how they can be saved."

Hidden Treasure Questions:

✔ How well do you know your Bible? Have you ever memorized verses of Scripture so you can share them with others?

✔ Have you ever thought, like the Ethiopian, that you would like to be baptized?

Listen to this story online!

Scan for bonus content

Simon the Sorcerer

This story is taken from Acts 8.

The Christians in Jerusalem were very sad that Stephen had been stoned to death. He was one of their greatest champions, but they should have expected it. Jesus had predicted that this kind of persecution would arise. "You will be brought before governors and kings for My sake, as a testimony to them and to the Gentiles," Jesus had said (Matthew 10:18).

The church continued to suffer persecution in Jerusalem, and after the stoning of Stephen things went from bad to worse. In fact, his death seemed to bring a whole new wave of persecution against the fledgling church. Saul, a member of the Sanhedrin, traveled far and wide making trouble for Christians, "entering every house, and dragging off men and women, committing them to prison" (Acts 8:3).

Some thought that the church would grow weaker because of

Simon himself also believed, and when he was baptized, he spent a lot of time with Philip.

Stephen's death, but they were wrong. Instead, it became stronger. Although many Christians were very discouraged when Stephen died, his blood became the seed of the young church. Many who witnessed Stephen's shining face at his execution desired to have that kind of peace in their hearts. Large numbers of priests also believed and were baptized.

However, it was not God's plan that the Christians should stay in Jerusalem forever. Jesus Himself had told them, "You shall receive power when the Holy Spirit has come upon you; and you shall be witnesses to Me in Jerusalem, and in all Judea and Samaria, and to the end of the earth" (Acts 1:8).

And so it was that the believers scattered everywhere. Some Christians went to Joppa and Caesarea along the coast, and others fled to Antioch, north of Galilee.

Philip went to Samaria and began preaching the gospel there. He was a very successful evangelist, and the reaction of the people in Samaria was amazing. Everyone believed his message of salvation because of all the miracles that he did. He cast out demons and healed those who were paralyzed and lame. The city had never seen anything like this, and they were so happy!

Now, there was a man in Samaria named Simon, who had practiced sorcery for years. He astonished the people of Samaria with his witchcraft and magic tricks and wanted everyone to think he was someone great. People listened to his advice as a fortune-teller. They even said, "This man has the power of God."

However, when they heard the things that Philip was preaching about Jesus Christ and the kingdom of God, many believed. They accepted the message and were baptized as Christians.

Then Simon himself also believed, and when he was baptized, he spent a lot of time with Philip. He saw all of the miracles and signs that Philip did and was amazed.

By now, the apostles in Jerusalem had heard about the excitement in Samaria. They learned that people believed the gospel story and were being baptized. So Peter and John were sent to see for themselves.

When they arrived in Samaria, they found it was all true. When the two apostles laid hands on the new believers and prayed for them, the Holy Spirit came upon them all.

Simon saw what Peter and John did, and he offered them money to be able to do things like that. "Give me this power also, that anyone on whom I lay hands may receive the Holy Spirit," he said.

Peter was upset that Simon would say such a thing. "Your money perish with you," he replied, "because you thought that the gift of God could be purchased with money! You have neither part nor portion in this matter, for your heart is not right in the sight of God. Repent therefore of this wickedness, and pray to God, and perhaps this thought of your heart may be forgiven you. For I see that you are poisoned by bitterness and bound by iniquity."

Simon saw his mistake immediately. "Pray to the Lord for me that none of the things which you have spoken may come upon me," he said.

Peter and John continued to meet with the believers in Samaria for several days to encourage them.

Then they returned to Jerusalem and preached the gospel in many villages of the Samaritans along the way. God was with them, and large numbers were added to the church every day.

> **Simon saw what Peter and John did, and he offered them money to be able to do things like that.**

Our Prayer:

"Dear Heavenly Father, help me to stay away from all kinds of magic and sorcery, even if people say they are using it for Jesus."

Hidden Treasure Questions:

✔ Who became a successful evangelist in Samaria?

✔ Why did Peter scold Simon the sorcerer?

Listen to this story online!

Scan for bonus content

From Persecutor to Preacher

This story is taken from Acts 9 and
The Acts of the Apostles, chapter 12.

Saul of Tarsus was becoming a champion for the Jewish leaders in Jerusalem. He had been the lawyer to stand up at Stephen's trial and convince everyone that Stephen was a blasphemer. He had even watched Stephen being stoned. But Stephen's execution troubled him afterward, and he wondered if they were right in treating Christians that way.

Finally, he went to talk about it to the chief priests, but they convinced him that Stephen was indeed a blasphemer of God and that he deserved to be stoned for it. Saul respected these leaders a lot. When he finally decided that they were right, he became the Christians' most bitter enemy in Jerusalem. He was not afraid to hunt down the followers of Jesus, even going door-to-door to find them. Sometimes he even barged into their homes at night to drag them away to prison.

But persecuting the Christians in Jerusalem wasn't enough for Saul. He wanted to go abroad to find them in other cities where they had likely fled. Damascus, for example, was next on his list.

So he went to the high priest and asked for official letters that he could take to the rabbis and elders in the Jewish synagogue at Damascus. If he found any followers of Jesus in the community there, he would bring them in chains to Jerusalem.

The trip to Damascus was a hot, dry one over wilderness roads. After many days of travel, Saul and his companions were looking forward to the refreshing rest they would get when they got to the city. About noon on the last day of their journey, when they were within sight of the city, something strange happened that changed Saul's life forever.

Suddenly a light brighter than the noonday

Persecuting the Christians in Jerusalem wasn't enough for Saul.

As Saul lay there in confusion and fear, he heard a voice saying to him, "Saul, Saul, why are you persecuting Me?"

sun shone all around Saul. The glorious light was too much for human eyes to bear, and he fell to the ground.

As he lay there in confusion and fear, he heard a voice saying to him, "Saul, Saul, why are you persecuting Me?"

"Who are You, Lord?" was all Saul could say.

"I am Jesus, whom you are persecuting," came the voice again. His companions were blinded by the light and speechless. They heard a voice, but saw no one. However, Saul knew who was talking to him. He had been persecuting the followers of Jesus continually, and now he was sure that Jesus had come to punish him for it.

In fear and trembling he lay on the ground. "Lord, what do You want me to do?" he asked.

"Arise and go into the city, and you will be told what you must do," the Lord replied.

Then Saul got up from the ground, but he couldn't see. Those who were with him had to lead him by the hand into Damascus.

He was very upset over what had happened and wouldn't eat or drink for three days. He kept thinking of what Jesus had said. Was it possible that by persecuting Jesus' followers he was not serving God, but Satan? He had been so sure that the scribes and priests in Jerusalem were right when they said that Jesus' resurrection was just a story created by the disciples. But now that he had spoken with Jesus, he would never be the same.

In Damascus at this time there was a follower of Jesus named Ananias. The Lord came to him in a vision and said, "Arise and go to the street called Straight. Inquire at the house of Judas for one called Saul of Tarsus, for behold, he is praying. In a vision he has seen a man named Ananias coming in and putting his hand on him, so that he might receive his sight."

As we can imagine, Ananias was frightened and didn't want to obey God's command. "Lord, I have heard from many about this man, how much harm he has done to Your saints in Jerusalem," said Ananias. "And here, he has authority from the chief priests to bind all who call on Your name."

But the Lord insisted, "Go, for he is a chosen vessel of Mine to bear My name before Gentiles, kings, and the children of Israel. For I will show him how many things he must suffer for My name's sake."

So Ananias did as he was told. He went to the street called Straight, entered the house where Saul was staying, and laid his hands on him. "Brother Saul, the Lord Jesus, who appeared to you on the road as you came, has sent me that you may receive your sight and be filled with the Holy Spirit."

Suddenly it seemed to Saul that something like scales fell from his eyes, and he could see again. The whole thing must have been a very frightening experience, but Saul was very glad to have his eyesight back.

So it was that Saul was baptized and became a Christian. The man who had hunted Christians down now became one of them himself.

When he had eaten some food, he was strengthened.

Then he wanted to spend some time with the disciples at Damascus, and his message in the synagogues was "Christ, the Son of God." Of course, everyone who heard him was amazed and very suspicious. Was this some kind of trick? they wondered. "Isn't this the man who destroyed those who called on God's name in Jerusalem?" they asked. "No doubt he has come here for that purpose, so that he might bring them bound to the chief priests."

Suddenly it seemed to Saul that something like scales fell from his eyes, and he could see again.

But the Jews were even more unhappy with Saul. He had been their best champion against the Christians, and they now plotted to kill him.

Evil men were sent to watch the gates of Damascus to catch him, but the Christian believers found out about their plot. While the enemies of Saul waited, the believers took him by night and let him down in a large basket through a hole in the city wall.

When Saul arrived back in Jerusalem, he went to see all the disciples, but they were afraid of him. No one believed that he had become a follower of Jesus. However, Barnabas took him to the apostles and told them about Saul's conversion story. Jesus had appeared to Saul on the road to Damascus, and now Saul was a changed man. He had given his heart to God.

So it was that Saul the persecutor of Jesus' followers became Saul the great soul winner for Jesus.

Our Prayer:

"Dear Jesus, please forgive me when I am mean. I hope I never treat anyone as badly as Saul did."

Hidden Treasure Questions:

✔ Why did the Jews hate the Christians so much?

✔ At the gates of what town did Saul meet Jesus in a vision?

Listen to this story online!

Scan for bonus content

Dorcas Raised to Life

This story is taken from Acts 9 and
The Acts of the Apostles, chapter 14.

The story of Jesus' death and resurrection was being told everywhere. People couldn't believe that God would come to earth to live and then die for the human race. The love and goodness of God, as shown in the life of Jesus, was now the most popular story anywhere. It seemed too good to be true. However, when people heard the message, and saw the astounding miracles that the disciples were doing through the power of the Holy Spirit, they believed. The gospel was transforming lives and making people more like Jesus.

At that time, the work was spreading so fast and had now reached the cities along the coast. One story in the town of Lydda told how Peter had healed a man named Aeneas, who had been in bed paralyzed for eight years.

Such a thing must have been a shock and a real blessing to the people in Lydda! In fact, the Bible says that everyone was surprised when they heard about the miracle. And because of it, they believed in Peter's message and turned to the Lord.

In Joppa, another city along the coast not far away, there was a woman named Tabitha who had accepted the story of salvation. She had another name, Dorcas, and that is the name we know her by. The Bible tells us that she was a kind, gentle woman who was always doing nice things for others.

Dorcas was a minister. Sometimes when we think of ministers, we think of people who go around preaching in strong, loud voices to large groups of people. Some ministers do that, and by the power of God many people are led to Christ and a great work is done.

But all great ministers are not preachers. Dorcas would see someone in need and make them clothing. Or she would see someone hungry and fix them some food. Her needle and thread and stove preached a better sermon than her mouth. She ministered to the people in the same way that Jesus did when He was on this earth. A bowl of food for the hungry, or a coat for those who are cold, is just as important as preaching the gospel. Dorcas was indeed a great minister.

> **Dorcas would see someone in need and make them clothing. Or she would fix them some food.**

Then one day something terrible happened. Dorcas became very sick and died. Everyone who knew her in Joppa was stunned. They probably asked one another again and again why God would allow such a good woman to be taken from them like that. She was a wonderful person and had done so much good!

With great sadness, the believers in that town prepared her for burial and laid her in an upper room. Someone said that Peter was in Joppa at the time, so they decided to send two men to get him.

"Come quickly," the messengers told Peter. In those days, people had to be buried the same day that they died because the body would begin to decay very quickly.

Peter came immediately and found the believers mourning for her as though their hearts would break. Everyone stood around weeping and showing Peter the clothes that Dorcas had made for them while she was living.

Peter was in the habit of listening to the voice of God. And he was impressed that he should send the mourners out of the room. Then he knelt down to pray and ask God to do something very special. Dorcas had been such a blessing to the church members in Joppa, and Peter now asked God to bring her back to life. After he finished praying, Peter said, "Tabitha, arise."

And through the power of God, she opened her eyes. Then Peter took her by the hand and lifted her up. He called all of the believers into the room, and they probably all started crying again, except this time they were tears of joy. Dorcas was alive! They had never seen anything so amazing, and everyone began praising God.

Dorcas had been such a blessing to the church members in Joppa, and Peter now asked God to bring her back to life.

The story of this miracle spread like a wildfire throughout Joppa and to nearby towns, and many believed in the Lord.

The resurrection of Dorcas is an example of what it will be like someday for those who are raised to eternal life when Jesus comes again. In that glorious morning, Jesus will tell everyone who has labored in service for Him, "Well done, good and faithful servant." I want to hear those words; don't you?

Our Prayer:

"Thank You, Jesus, for this inspiring story! I know that someday soon You will come again and raise to life all of those such as Dorcas who have served You faithfully."

Hidden Treasure Questions:

✔ What was Dorcas' real name?

✔ What kinds of things had Dorcas done for the Christian believers in Joppa?

Listen to this story online!

Scan for bonus content

Peter and the Sheet

This story is taken from Acts 10 and
The Acts of the Apostles, chapter 14.

There was a centurion living in Caesarea whose name was Cornelius. He and his family were sincere in their worship of God. Although they didn't know anything about Jesus, Cornelius gave some of his money to help the poor, and he was a man of prayer.

One day about three o'clock in the afternoon, while he was praying, an angel of God came to him in a vision. "Cornelius, God hears your prayers and sees the good things you have done to help the poor," the angel said. "Now send men to Joppa to get Simon, whose surname is Peter. He is lodging with a man named Simon, a tanner, whose house is by the sea. He will tell you what you must do."

There was a centurion living in Caesarea whose name was Cornelius. He and his family were sincere in their worship of God.

When the angel left, Cornelius called for two of his servants and a loyal soldier who was with him all the time. He told them the message from the angel. Then he sent them on their way to look for Simon Peter in Joppa.

It was nearly a full day's journey for the servants of Cornelius. They probably had to stay somewhere for the night, but the next day they hurried on their way, nearing the city of Joppa about noon.

Meanwhile, Peter was at Simon the tanner's house waiting to eat the midday meal. He went up on the rooftop to spend some time in prayer, and God sent him a vision. In the vision he saw heaven opened and something like a big sheet tied at its four corners coming down to earth. In the sheet were all kinds of wild animals, creepy-crawly things, and birds.

Suddenly Peter heard a voice say to him, "Rise, Peter; kill and eat."

Now, that must have seemed like a very strange thing for Peter to hear. "Who would ever want to eat such unclean, smelly creatures?" he must have thought to himself as the vision ended.

"I can't do that, Lord!" Peter protested. "I have never eaten anything common or unclean."

"What God has cleansed you must not call common," the voice added.

This same vision came to Peter three times, and each time the sheet was drawn back up to heaven from where it had come.

Peter was confused about the vision and was wondering what it could mean when suddenly the messengers from Cornelius arrived at the house. While they were at the front gate asking if there was a Simon Peter lodging there, the Holy Spirit told him, "Behold, three men are seeking you. Arise, go down, and go with them, doubting nothing, for I have sent them."

And so Peter went down and greeted them, saying, "I am Peter. I am the one you are looking for. For what reason have you come?"

The men were probably relieved to find Peter after coming so far. They told him, "Cornelius the centurion has sent us to find you. He is a just man, one who fears God and has a good reputation among all the nation of the Jews. He was divinely instructed by a holy angel to call you to his house and to hear words from you."

Peter welcomed them in, giving them food and a place to stay for the night. The next day he returned to Caesarea with them, taking with him several Christian brothers from Joppa.

When the group arrived at Cornelius' house in Caesarea, the centurion was waiting for them with all his relatives and close friends. And when Peter came in, he knelt at his feet and worshipped him.

But Peter took Cornelius by the hand and lifted him up, saying, "Stand up, for I myself am also a man like you."

When Peter saw all the people who had gathered together, he said, "You know how unlawful it is for a Jewish man to keep company with someone of another nation. But God has shown me that I should not call any man common or unclean. Therefore, I came without objection as soon as I was sent for. I ask, then, for what reason have you sent for me?"

In a vision Peter saw heaven opened and a big sheet tied at the four corners coming down to earth. In the sheet were all kinds of wild animals, creepy-crawly things, and birds.

Cornelius replied, "Four days ago I was fasting until this hour. At the ninth hour, (3:00 p.m.) I prayed in my house, and behold, a man stood before me in bright clothing. He said, 'Cornelius, your prayer has been heard, and your offerings to the poor are remembered in the sight of God. Send therefore to Joppa and call Simon here, whose surname is Peter. He is lodging in the house of Simon, a tanner, by the sea. When he comes, he will speak to you.' So I sent to you immediately, and you have done well to come. Now therefore, we are all present before God to hear all the things commanded you by God."

Peter was surprised that God would ask him to come to preach the gospel to a man like Cornelius, who was not a Jew. It was not the custom for Jewish Christians to even go into the house of a man who was not a Jew. However, because of the angel and the vision he had been given, he knew that it was God's wish that he do so.

"Now I know that God plays no favorites when it comes to the gospel," Peter said. "He has righteous people in every nation who fear Him, and He accepts them as they are. The word which God sent to the children of Israel through Jesus Christ has been proclaimed throughout all Judea. It began in Galilee after Jesus of Nazareth was baptized and God anointed Him with the power of the Holy Spirit. He went about doing good and healing all who were oppressed by the devil, for God was with Him. He is Lord of all, and we are witnesses of all things which He did in the land of the Jews and in Jerusalem."

He continued to explain, "They killed Him by hanging Him on a tree, but God raised Him up on the third day and showed Him openly. He did not appear to all the people, but to witnesses chosen by God, even to us who ate and drank with Him after He arose from the dead. And He commanded us to preach to the people and to tell them that it is He who was ordained by God to be Judge of the living and the dead. To Him all the prophets witness that, through His name, whoever believes in Him will receive forgiveness of sins."

Peter said, "God has righteous people in every nation who fear Him, and He accepts them."

While Peter was still speaking to Cornelius and those who were with him in the house, the Holy Spirit suddenly came upon them. Peter and the Jewish believers who had come with him were astonished!

They had never seen the gift of the Holy Spirit given to a Gentile. However, here they were praising God and speaking in languages they didn't know, just like Peter and the other disciples had on the Day of Pentecost.

"Can anyone say that these Gentiles should not be baptized with water?" Peter said. "After all, they have received the Holy Spirit just as we have."

And so they baptized them all in the name of the Lord, and there was much rejoicing in the house of Cornelius.

Our Prayer:

"Dear God, I pray that I will be willing to share the gospel with anyone You ask me to."

Hidden Treasure Questions:

✓ Who told Cornelius that he should send for Peter?

✓ What was the vision about that Peter had while he was waiting to eat?

Listen to this story online!

Scan for bonus content

Chained Between Two Soldiers

This story is taken from Acts 12 and *The Acts of the Apostles*, chapter 15.

The Christian church was under fire now. The small group of believers had grown to several thousand in the 13 short years since Jesus had gone back to heaven, and that didn't make the Jewish leaders in Jerusalem too happy. In fact, it was their wish to stamp out the very life of the young church before it could get started.

Herod Agrippa wasn't helping any. Hoping to make peace with the Jewish Sanhedrin in Jerusalem, he began arresting some of the Christian leaders. James, the brother of John, was one of the first. Without a fair trial Herod ordered James to be executed with the sword, and then he turned his attention on Peter.

Herod soon found Peter and locked him up in prison at the Roman garrison. He handed Peter over to four sets of guards to guard him around the clock. In the deepest chambers of the prison Peter was kept chained between two guards, and two more guards were standing directly outside his cell.

The annual Passover Feast had just begun, and Herod was a bit worried. The leaders at the Sanhedrin would have liked to see Peter killed right away, but Herod had other ideas. Not wanting to risk a possible riot on such a big public holiday, he decided to put

Herod soon found Peter and locked him up in prison.

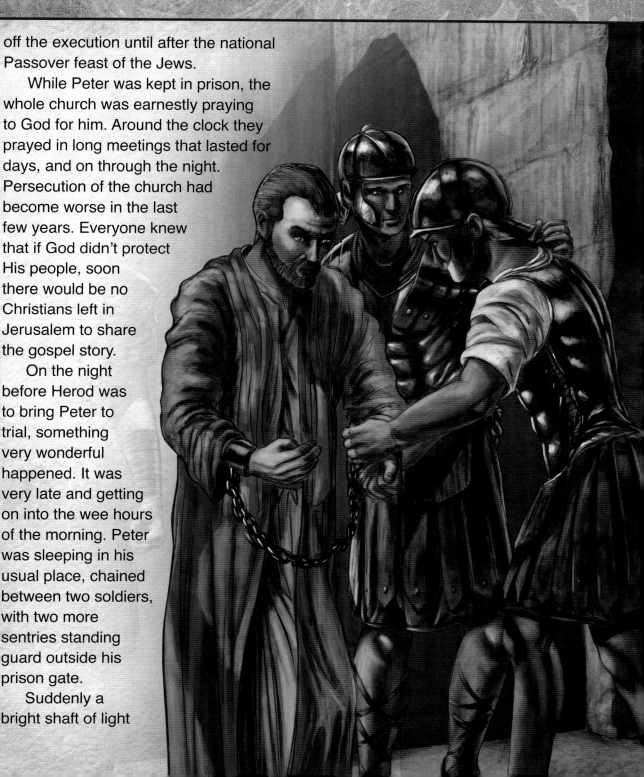

off the execution until after the national Passover feast of the Jews.

While Peter was kept in prison, the whole church was earnestly praying to God for him. Around the clock they prayed in long meetings that lasted for days, and on through the night. Persecution of the church had become worse in the last few years. Everyone knew that if God didn't protect His people, soon there would be no Christians left in Jerusalem to share the gospel story.

On the night before Herod was to bring Peter to trial, something very wonderful happened. It was very late and getting on into the wee hours of the morning. Peter was sleeping in his usual place, chained between two soldiers, with two more sentries standing guard outside his prison gate.

Suddenly a bright shaft of light

pierced the darkness as an angel came to stand by Peter's side. His brilliant glory chased away the darkness of the prison cell. Strangely enough, the guards in the cell were not awakened. In fact, they continued sleeping the whole time, as if they were in a drunken stupor.

"Get up, quick!" the angel said as he touched Peter and awakened him with a start. Of course, Peter could not believe his eyes. "I must be dreaming," he thought as he squinted at the brightness of the angel's light.

Suddenly a bright shaft of light pierced the darkness as an angel came to stand by Peter's side.

"Put on your clothes and sandals," the angel said, and magically the chains on Peter's wrists fell off. "Wrap your cloak around yourself and follow me!"

Peter obeyed the angel and followed him out of the prison and away from the two guards between whom he had been chained. He went right past the two sentries standing guard just outside his cell, past the rest of the prison guards, and through the iron outer gate that opened onto the street.

By the time they were out on the street, Peter was wide awake. Could this really be happening? he must have wondered over and over again, as he stared at the angel. "Has God actually sent His angel to free me from prison and certain death?" Maybe this was a vision from God.

The two of them walked the full length of one street until they were far from the prison, and then the angel disappeared as quickly as he had come.

"Thank You, Father," Peter prayed. "Now I know without a doubt that the Lord has sent His angel and rescued me from Herod's clutches. He has delivered me from everything the Jewish people were planning to do."

Sneaking up one street and down another, Peter was making his way to Mary's house. She was the mother of John Mark, and as usual was providing a meeting place for everyone. On this night in particular lots of Christians were there praying around the clock for Peter. We can almost hear some of them saying, "It could be that God will perform one of His miracles for us."

When he arrived at the outer gate, he knocked repeatedly, until Rhoda, a servant girl, came to the door. "It's Peter," she said. I can hear him saying, "Open up; it's cold out here!"

She did not open the door, but when she recognized his voice she ran very excitedly back into the house, where they were still praying. "Peter is at the door!"

she exclaimed in a half whisper. "You're crazy," many told her. "He can't be at the door! He's in prison! It must be his angel!"

But she insisted, and he kept knocking. Soon there was nothing left for them to do but go and see who was at the door. Imagine their surprise when they opened the door to see Peter standing there! They must have been very excited, as everyone began talking at once. We can be sure there was lots of hugging, crying, and thanking God that Peter was safe at last.

"Peter is at the door!" she exclaimed in a half-whisper. "You are crazy," many told her.

Sooner or later, though, Peter must have held up his hand for silence, and then he told them the whole story of how God had delivered him from prison. Maybe he even quoted Psalm 34:7 for them. "The angel of the Lord encamps all around those who fear Him, and delivers them."

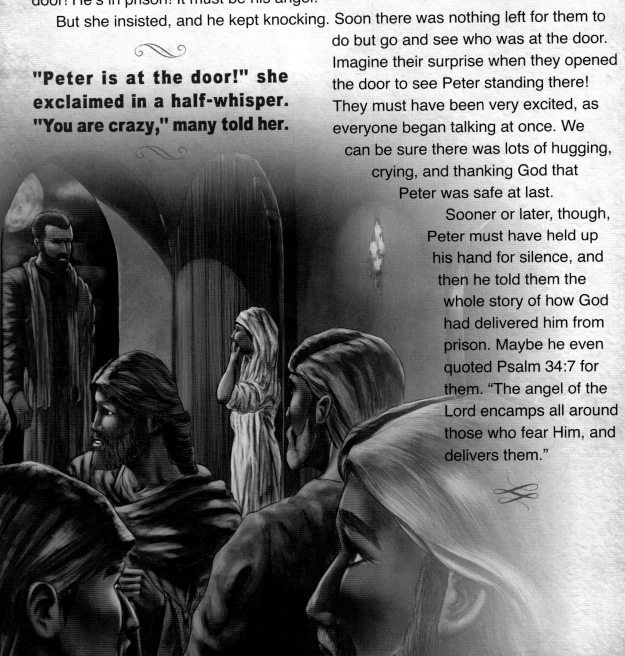

Our Prayer:

"Help me to be faithful to You, Lord, even though I may someday have to go to prison for it."

Hidden Treasure Questions:

✔ Peter was faithful to God even though it nearly cost him his life. Could you do the same?

✔ Someday, before Jesus comes, your angel may deliver you from a dangerous place such as what happened to Peter. What are you doing to prepare for that day?

Listen to this story online!

Scan for bonus content

Adventures in Antioch

This story is taken from Acts 11 and 13 and
The Acts of the Apostles, chapters 16 and 17.

For many years after Jesus went back to heaven, most of the new Christians who became followers of Jesus had been Jews. The Jews were already looking for the Messiah, who was to become the Savior of the world, so they seemed the most likely to accept the teachings of Jesus. They also understood that the Scriptures were the Word of God, that God's rest day was the Sabbath, and that there was only one true God. However, when Cornelius and his family in Caesarea were baptized, a new day began for the church. Now it was becoming clearer that God wanted them to take the gospel to the Gentiles, too. Of course, this made sense to them when they really thought about it. After all, Jesus had said that the story of salvation must go to all the world.

Not everyone agreed on this, and there was a big discussion about it when Peter went back to Jerusalem to share the story of Cornelius' conversion. The leaders were surprised to hear that Peter had even eaten with Cornelius and his family. This was never done, because it was thought that Jews would become defiled and less spiritual somehow by doing such things. As far as they were concerned, salvation was for the Jews only, because they were God's chosen people.

But no one could deny the fact that God was indeed pouring out His Holy Spirit on the Gentiles. Peter's vision and the amazing events at the home of Cornelius proved that. It was clear that God wanted the gospel to go to both Jews and Gentiles.

Now groups of Christian believers were beginning to pop up everywhere, with both Jews and Gentiles in the churches. Persecution in Jerusalem had forced the Christians to flee to foreign cities, and Antioch was one such place. It was a tourist town with a pleasant climate and lots of people coming and going all the time. It was the perfect place for the gospel to be preached, and the workers there were having great success in winning people to Jesus.

Peter went back to Jerusalem to share the story of Cornelius' conversion. The leaders were surprised to hear that Peter had even eaten with Cornelius.

It was in Antioch that the believers were first called Christians. One of the believers named Barnabas was especially blessed by God as he worked with both Jews and Gentiles. The Bible says that he was a good man, full of the Holy Spirit and faith.

However, he felt that he needed another strong believer to help him lead the new group of followers in that famous city. So he went looking for Saul and found him in his hometown of Tarsus. He knew that Saul was a new believer, a talented speaker, and very excited to be preaching the Word of God.

The two men became a great team, and the church grew by leaps and bounds. New converts were being won to Jesus every week, it seemed. God was doing great things among the new Christians, and they were a generous group. When a prophet named Agabus came from Jerusalem predicting a severe famine, the believers in Antioch took up a large collection and sent it back to help the believers in Judea.

One day as the church group was fasting and praying, the Holy Spirit came upon them with a new idea. "I want Barnabas and Saul to work together," said the Holy Spirit. So the believers laid hands on the two men to dedicate them, and then sent them away as missionaries. Saul was being called Paul now, and he and Barnabas made a great team. John Mark also went along, and they all sailed off to the island of Cyprus.

Elymas was a bad influence on Sergius Paulus and turned him away from the message.

When they reached the island, they met a Jewish sorcerer named Elymas. He worked with Sergius Paulus, the proconsul of the island, who wished to hear the Word of God.

But Elymas was a bad influence on Sergius Paulus and turned him away from the message Paul and Barnabas were preaching. When Paul realized this, the Holy Spirit came upon him with a special message for Elymas. "You son of the devil," he said, "why are you perverting the straight ways of the Lord? Because of this, you shall now be blind for a while."

Everyone must have been shocked to hear Paul say such a thing, but when Elymas suddenly became blind, they could see that it was God's doing.

Fortunately, this story has a happy ending. Sergius Paulus was amazed when he saw the power of God and became a believer in the gospel message preached by Paul and Barnabas.

Our Prayer:

"Dear Jesus, help me to be a faithful missionary for You wherever I go."

Hidden Treasure Questions:

✔ Who joined Paul and Barnabas when they went to the island of Cyprus?

✔ What was the name of the sorcerer who was a bad influence on Sergius Paulus?

Listen to this story online!

Scan for bonus content

An Angry Mob Stones Paul

This story is taken from Acts 14 and
The Acts of the Apostles, chapter 18.

Paul and Barnabas had been traveling together ever since the Holy Spirit had asked them to partner up as missionaries. They both had the same goal, and that was to do what Jesus had told them to do: "Go into all the world and preach the gospel to every creature" (Mark 16:15). Every time they entered a city, their message was the same. They would preach the good news of a risen Savior.

When they went to the city of Iconium, in what is today the country of Turkey, they worshipped at the synagogue of the Jews, as had been their custom. They were good speakers, and their preaching was so convincing that the Jews and the Greeks believed their message about the gospel of Jesus.

However, the unbelieving Jews poisoned their minds toward Paul and Barnabas and made a lot of trouble for them in the city. At first this did not discourage the two missionaries, and they continued to preach boldly. They also did many miraculous signs and wonders among the people.

Barnabas they called Zeus, and Paul was called Hermes. Then they called for the priest from the temple of Zeus and brought oxen and wreaths of flowers to the city gates.

Unfortunately, things didn't go as well as they had hoped. Because of all the trouble the Jewish leaders were giving them, the people in the synagogue were divided. Some sided with the Jewish leaders and some with Paul and Barnabas.

Finally, friends warned Paul and Barnabas about a secret plot to kill them. Only then did the two missionaries decide to leave, and off they went to the city of Lystra. This city was ready for a message of hope such as the one that Paul and Barnabas were bringing, and soon they were preaching in the synagogue.

One day while Paul was preaching, he noticed a crippled man, who had been lame since birth. Paul was impressed that the man had the faith he needed to be healed, so he commanded him to stand up.

Immediately, the man jumped to his feet and began walking. The crowds listening to Paul preach got very excited when they saw the miracle, and news of it spread all over town. Soon the Gentiles were all shouting, "The gods have come down to us in the likeness of men!"

Barnabas they called Zeus, and Paul was called Hermes, because he was the

The mob went wild and attacked the two men. Paul was beaten badly as the mob began throwing stones at him.

main speaker for the two of them. Then they called for the priest from the temple of Zeus and brought oxen and wreaths of flowers to the city gates. With these, they hoped to make a public sacrifice in honor of the amazing miracle that these men had done.

When Barnabas and Paul realized what was happening, they tore their clothes to show how upset they were. Then they ran into the crowd shouting, "Men, why are you doing these things? We also are men with the same nature as you, and preach to you that you should turn from these useless things to the living God, who made the heaven, the earth, the sea, and all things that are in them."

But no one seemed to be listening, and the two missionaries could hardly keep the crowd from going through with the sacrifice.

However, Jews from Antioch and Iconium showed up, and that spelled trouble. When they heard that Paul was in town and had done an amazing miracle, they were very jealous. They knew that Paul had once been their best champion against Christians. The fact that he was now a Christian himself and winning souls to Jesus right and left made them angry, and they decided to turn the crowds against him.

They stirred up the

people of Lystra and persuaded them that Paul and Barnabas were scoundrels and up to no good. From that moment forward, things went from bad to worse, and the angry crowds quickly became a mob.

Satan was in that mob stirring things up. If he could get these people to reject the two missionaries before they really had a chance to hear their message, the door of salvation would close, at least for a while.

The mob went wild and attacked the two men. Paul was beaten badly as the mob began throwing stones at him. Stoning was a common way to execute people in those days.

There had been no trial. If the Roman authorities had known about it, they would not have been happy about the mob taking the law into its own hands. But the Jewish leaders were known for this kind of thing all over the world. Hadn't they crucified Jesus and many of His followers already?

How Barnabas escaped is a mystery, but by now, Paul was unconscious. Everybody thought he was dead, so they dragged him through the streets and tossed his body outside the city gates.

Satan was triumphant. He had once used Paul to kill Christians, and now he used an angry mob to kill Paul.

The believers in Lystra were devastated. They wondered, "How could God have allowed this to happen to such a great man?" And they gathered around Paul to weep and mourn.

But Paul wasn't dead. When he finally woke up, he got up, and went back to the city. It was a miracle, and the people were astonished!

Things had not gone well for Paul and Barnabas in Lystra, so they decided they would leave this city for a while. There would be time for them to come back again sometime in the future.

The next day they left for a city called Derbe. When they preached the gospel there, they were accepted and baptized many of the believers, who then became disciples for the church.

God blessed Paul and Barnabas in their travels, and they were able to return to all the churches that they had raised up along the way. In cities such as Lystra and Iconium, they again won many souls for Jesus, encouraging them to be faithful to God.

"Through many tribulations we must enter the kingdom of God," they told the people. Everyone knew that Paul and Barnabas had suffered much for the sake of the gospel, so they listened to them and believed.

Paul was unconscious. Everybody thought he was dead, so they tossed his body outside the city gates.

The two missionaries prayed with the people and organized the churches for service to God. They did this by appointing elders and other leaders to minister to the people until they themselves could return for another visit.

Finally, after months and months of laboring among the Gentiles, Paul and Barnabas came full circle in their travels. Once again, they returned to the church in Antioch, where they had first been dedicated as a missionary team. In that city, they gave a report to the Christians about how God had blessed them, and how He had opened the door of faith to the Gentiles.

So it was that the first missionary journey ended for Paul and Barnabas. And they continued in their habit of encouraging people to trust in Jesus and to help spread the gospel story everywhere.

Our Prayer:

"Dear God, help me to remember that sharing the gospel with others may bring me suffering sometimes, but it is worth it if I can win souls for You."

Hidden Treasure Questions:

✓ What were the names of some cities where Paul and Barnabas traveled in their journeys?

✓ What made the crowds in Lystra think Paul and Barnabas were gods?

Listen to this story online!

Scan for bonus content

Fighting in Church

This story is taken from Acts 15 and
The Acts of the Apostles, chapter 19.

In many of the towns where Paul and Barnabas traveled, a real battle was going on between the Jewish believers and the new Gentile converts. The Jews said that all Christians should continue to keep the rules that had been handed down to them from the law of Moses. These rules were more than just the Ten Commandments. Many of them were not even in the Bible, but were part of the Jewish traditions started since the Jews came back from their captivity in Babylon.

For example, the Jews had rules about washing their hands so that they could be clean spiritually. But the new Gentile converts had been baptized, and they were taking part in foot washing at the Communion services in their churches, just as Jesus had asked. Why did they need to wash their hands, too?

This caused trouble for the new Gentile believers. They knew nothing about the old covenants that God had made with the Israelite forefathers. They couldn't see what many of the old rules had to do with the gospel of Jesus.

Other rules had to do with things from the old covenants given to the Israelites through great men such as Abraham and Jacob. But God had now rejected the Jews from being His chosen people. When they had crucified Jesus, He had removed His blessings from them as a people and poured out His Holy Spirit on the new Christian church.

Finally, the church leaders in Jerusalem decided that Paul and Barnabas should come down for a meeting to discuss these things. At the meeting, all of the apostles and elders hoped that they would be able to talk about the problems and come up with a solution.

So Paul and Barnabas made the trip to Jerusalem, where they were welcomed by the church and all of its leaders. Everyone had heard about the miracles that God was doing for Paul and Barnabas in their work with Gentiles, and there was great rejoicing.

However, it wasn't long before Satan stirred things up among the leaders. When they started discussing the problems in the church, some said that the laws of Moses were the most important thing to remember. Others said that the teachings of Jesus were. It didn't matter to Satan who won the arguments. He just wanted them to fight and argue so they would forget why they were preaching the gospel in the first place.

Finally, Peter stood up in the meeting and said, "Brethren, you know that God has chosen some of us to go to the Gentiles that they should hear the word of the gospel and believe. God, who knows the heart, has given them the Holy Spirit just as He did to us, and made no distinction between them and us purifying their hearts by faith.

"Therefore, why do you test God by putting a yoke on the neck of the disciples which neither our fathers nor we were able to bear? We believe that through the grace of the Lord Jesus Christ, we shall be saved in the same manner as they."

Then Barnabas and Paul stood up and shared all the miracles and wonders that God was doing among the Gentiles. Their stories were inspiring. It was clear that God was blessing the work with the

The Jews had rules about washing their hands. But the new Gentile converts were taking part in foot washing.

new Gentile believers. It wouldn't be long before there were more Gentile converts to Christianity than Jewish ones. They could not expect people who were Gentiles to keep the Jewish religious laws. To most of the leaders in Jerusalem, this made sense.

> **James stood up and said, "The Scriptures have told us that even the Gentiles will be called by God's name."**

After much discussion and prayer, James stood up and said, "The Scriptures have told us that even the Gentiles will be called by God's name. Therefore, I judge that we should not trouble those from among the Gentiles who are turning to God. We should ask them to follow a few simple rules that are best for the whole church. For example, we should ask them not to eat any food that has been dedicated to pagan idols. We should also ask them to be sexually pure, and they should avoid eating the meat from animals that have been strangled."

And so it was that the first big meeting between all the church leaders ended, and God helped them solve their problems as they had prayed He would. The gospel continued to go the world, and the church was blessed in so many ways.

Our Prayer:

"Dear Jesus, thank You for helping Your people discuss things in a godly way so that Your work could go forward."

Hidden Treasure Questions:

✔ Why did the church leaders all meet in Jerusalem?

✔ What three basic rules did James suggest that all believers everywhere should follow?

Listen to this story online!

Scan for bonus content

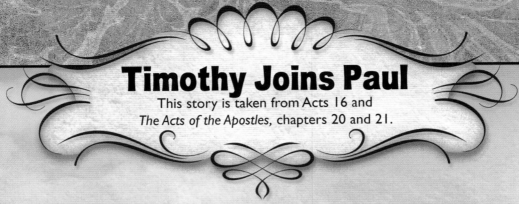

Timothy Joins Paul

This story is taken from Acts 16 and
The Acts of the Apostles, chapters 20 and 21.

Paul and Barnabas had been serving together for quite a while now, and they had just finished a missionary journey together. They had been sharing the gospel everywhere as they preached the stories of God's power among the Gentiles.

After the big meeting in Jerusalem, Paul said to Barnabas, "Let's go back and visit our brothers in every city where we have preached the word of the Lord and see how they are doing."

Barnabas was excited about the trip, but he wanted to take John Mark with them again. Unfortunately, John Mark's first trip with them on their missionary journey had not gone well, because he got homesick and left them when they were in Pamphylia. Being on the road all the time required bravery, faith, and a willingness to sacrifice.

Paul didn't want John Mark to go with them this time, but Barnabas insisted that he should. They argued about it so much that they finally agreed that they should separate. After praying about it with the leaders of the church, they chose other partners to travel with them. Barnabas took John Mark and sailed to Cyprus, while Paul chose Silas and left for Syria and Cilicia.

When Paul and Silas arrived in Lystra, they met a young disciple named Timothy. His mother was a Jewish believer, but his father was Greek. Everyone in the Lystra and Iconium churches spoke well of him. Paul was very impressed with Timothy and asked him to travel with them on their missionary journey. Timothy agreed.

It must have been very exciting for Timothy to travel with Paul and Silas, who were becoming quite famous in Christian churches everywhere. Paul took a special interest in training Timothy because he saw great potential in the young man. Paul liked him so much, in fact, that he began calling him his "own son in the faith." Timothy had a bright mind and was always eager to learn. Often they would talk about the Scriptures and the stories about all of the champions of the faith.

When Paul and Silas arrived in Lystra, they met a young disciple named Timothy.

The three of them traveled back through the towns and cities that Paul and Barnabas had visited on their first missionary journey, and what an encouragement they were to the believers. They also gave a report on what had been decided in the big church council in Jerusalem. Both Jews and Gentiles were to obey three simple rules in the church: no food or drink offered to idols, no meat that had been strangled, and no sexual immorality.

Therefore, the missionary team strengthened the churches in their faith, and the number of believers increased daily.

The three missionaries continued on their way through Phrygia and Galatia and then finally Troas. One night in Troas, while Paul was sleeping, God gave him a vision. In the vision, a man from Macedonia was looking at him and begging, "Come over to Macedonia and help us." So the next day, Paul and his two partners left immediately for Macedonia. If God wanted them in Macedonia, that was where they must go. The only questions in their minds were: Who was the man Paul had seen in vision, and would they meet him?

They sailed on a ship along the coast, passing many port cities until they reached Philippi. It had originally been a Roman colony, but now it was the most important city in that part of Macedonia. The Bible doesn't say why they chose to stop at Philippi, but they must have been impressed that God wanted them there.

The next day, Paul and his two partners left immediately for Macedonia.

The men stayed in Philippi for several days, because it seemed that there would be so many chances to share the gospel in the city. On Sabbath, they went down to the beautiful riverside to pray and worship. While there, they visited with several godly women who met at the river regularly. A woman by the name of Lydia heard them talking that first Sabbath. She made purple dye for a living, and she was a believer in the one true God.

As she listened to the things Paul was saying, the Lord opened her heart to the gospel story. She received the truth gladly, and she and her household decided to be baptized.

To show her appreciation for their kindness in bringing her the gospel, she invited the three men to stay at her house. What a blessing that must have been, and they would need it. Trouble was on the way again.

Our Prayer:

"Dear Jesus, inspire me to go on a missionary journey for You someday."

Hidden Treasure Questions:

✔ What was the name of the young man who joined Paul and Silas on their journey?

✔ What did Lydia do for a living?

Listen to this story online!

Scan for bonus content

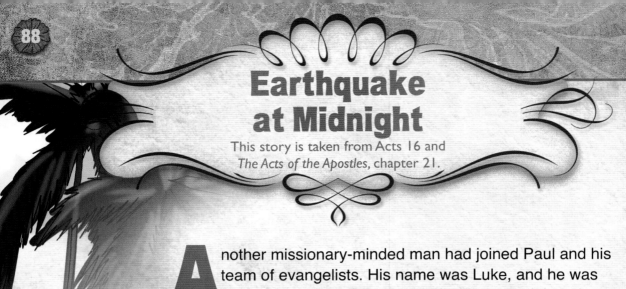

Earthquake at Midnight

This story is taken from Acts 16 and
The Acts of the Apostles, chapter 21.

Another missionary-minded man had joined Paul and his team of evangelists. His name was Luke, and he was a doctor of medicine. Imagine that! Paul and the other missionaries had their very own private physician ready to tend to them if they should get sick.

One day as Paul and his missionary companions were on their way to a prayer meeting, they noticed a young woman following them. She was obviously possessed by an evil spirit because she kept calling out in a loud voice, "These men are the servants of the Most High God, who proclaim to us the way of salvation."

It was sad to see this young woman under the power of Satan. To make matters worse, she was a slave. She brought her masters a lot of money in the business of fortune-telling, something that was very common in the days of the Romans.

When the masters of the slave girl saw that she was acting normal again and was no longer possessed, they were furious!

For several days, Paul suffered through such treatment, as the woman followed them everywhere. She was such a distraction because of all of her yelling. Imagine trying to preach or even have a conversation with someone when someone is interrupting you constantly.

Finally, Paul couldn't stand it any longer. Turning to the girl, he said to the spirit, "I command you in the name of Jesus Christ to come out of her." And that very hour the spirit came out. With the girl now in her right mind, she chose to become a follower of Christ.

When the masters of the slave girl saw that she was acting normal again and was no longer possessed, they were furious! Now she wouldn't earn them money as a fortune-teller. They grabbed Paul and Silas and dragged them into the marketplace to the authorities.

"These men are Jews and are making trouble in our city," they told the magistrates. "They teach customs that are not lawful for us, as Romans, to receive or observe."

By now, a mob had gathered. The confusion was so great that the local magistrates thought Paul and Silas must be some kind of serious criminals. Without even giving them a trial, the magistrates tore off their clothes and ordered that they be beaten with rods.

We can only imagine Paul and Silas gritting their teeth in pain as they prayed for strength and patience. After all, Jesus had suffered too. He had been beaten, spat upon, and then crucified. He went through all of this so that you and I could take part in His plan of salvation. If Jesus was willing to suffer so that they could be saved, then Paul and Silas were willing to suffer for Christ.

After the severe beating that Paul and Silas received, the magistrates locked them up in prison and commanded the jailer to keep them secure. The jailer must have thought that they were dangerous criminals, because he put them in a cell way down inside the prison and locked their feet in the stocks. What an experience! They were serving Jesus by bringing the light of the gospel to people who were lost in their sins, and they were suffering for it! But they didn't blame God. They knew that Satan was the cause for all their troubles. Satan is never happy when we are doing what Jesus wants us to do. When we follow the leading of Jesus, Satan does everything he can to make us stop. That is why Paul and Silas were beaten and put in prison.

To keep up their spirits, Paul and Silas began singing hymns to God. We can imagine all the other prisoners leaning as far as they could in the direction of the music coming from down in the deepest dungeon. They sang all evening, and probably even quoted a few Scripture verses.

Then suddenly at midnight, there was a

> To keep up their spirits, Paul and Silas began singing hymns to God.

big earthquake. It was so severe that the foundations of the prison shook, and within seconds, all of the prison doors opened. And all of the prisoners' chains were loosened. This would have been a good time to escape, but no one made a move. An unseen force had kept all the prisoners in place.

The keeper of the prison awakened from a deep sleep, and when he saw all of those prison doors open, he panicked. Every criminal in the prison was under his care, and now he thought that they had all escaped. If even one had escaped, he knew his own life would end for sure. That was the Roman law for officers in charge of prisons.

So he did the honorable thing. He drew the sword from his side and was ready to execute himself when he heard shouting. "Do yourself no harm!" Paul called out to the jailer. "We are all here!"

Then the jailer called for a light and ran into the innermost cell where he had locked up Paul and Silas. In amazement, he fell to his knees, trembling before them. "Sirs, what must I do to be saved?" he asked.

Paul and Silas replied, "Believe on the Lord Jesus Christ, and you will be saved, you and your household."

Then the jailer took them out of the prison and into his own house. He then washed the wounds on their backs, gave them food, and even introduced the two prisoners to his family.

Paul and Silas shared the story of salvation with the jailer and his family, including the hope of eternal life that is possible only in Jesus. Then the jailer and his family were all baptized, and they rejoiced because they now believed in the one true God.

The next morning the magistrates sent officers to the prison ordering the release of Paul and Silas. "Let those men go," they said.

The keeper of the prison passed the message on to Paul and Silas. "Now therefore depart, and go in peace," he said.

But Paul said, "Absolutely not! They have beaten us openly as uncondemned Romans, and have thrown us into prison. Now they want to put us out secretly? Definitely not! Let them come themselves and get us out."

The magistrates were very afraid when they heard that Paul and Silas were Roman citizens by birth, and they came personally to escort them to the city gate.

What a story for all of us to remember when we go through hard times! Someday we may have to face trials for our faith in Jesus such as Paul and Silas did. When that time comes, Jesus will help us to be faithful to God.

"Do yourself no harm!" Paul called out to the jailer. "We are all here!"

Our Prayer:

"Dear God, help me to be as cheerful as
Paul and Silas were, even when things go wrong."

Hidden Treasure Questions:

✔ Why were the owners of the slave girl
angry when Paul cast her demon out?

✔ What did Paul and Silas do while
they were in prison to keep their
spirits up?

Listen to this story online!

Scan for bonus content

They Turned the World Upside Down!

This story is taken from Acts 17 and
The Acts of the Apostles, chapter 22.

Paul and Silas had experienced some pretty amazing things in Philippi. However, the magistrates were afraid that there might be further trouble, so they sent the two missionaries on their way in peace. After their prison experience in Philippi, Paul and Silas decided to stop at Thessalonica. While they were there, they met a good man named Jason, who offered to let them stay at his house.

In this city, there were large Jewish synagogues, and Paul and Silas were given a chance to speak to the people on the Sabbath day. The people in the synagogue could tell that they had been mistreated and beaten, so Paul told them what had happened to them in Philippi.

But it was Paul's message of salvation that really interested the worshippers, and he was invited to come back to worship again and again to teach them from the Scriptures.

For three Sabbaths, he explained why Jesus had come to earth, and why He had to suffer and die. He told them that the Savior of the world had risen from the dead, and that those who believed in Him could have the hope of eternal life. "This Jesus whom I preach to you is the Christ," he said.

Paul also told the Thessalonians about his life as a persecutor of Christians in Judea. He had been a proud man who thought that doing good works could save him. However, his conversion experience on the road to Damascus changed all that. Jesus Christ had appeared to him as the promised Messiah and the Son of God.

> **For three Sabbaths, Paul explained why Jesus had come to earth, and why He had to suffer and die.**

Many in the synagogue were persuaded that Paul's words were from God. A large number of Greeks who were searching for truth formed the church group in that city. They were joined by many leading women in Thessalonica.

However, many Jews who listened to Paul in the synagogue were not convinced that his words were from God. They became envious of his popularity with the people. Leading a mob of evil men from the marketplace, they set the whole town in an uproar. Then they went to the house where Paul and Silas were staying.

But they didn't find them there. The crowd was so angry that they dragged Jason before the rulers of the city. "These who have turned the world upside down have come here, too!" they shouted. "Jason has harbored two strangers in his home, and these are all acting contrary to the decrees of Caesar, saying that there is another king, and that His name is Jesus."

The rulers of the city were troubled when they heard these things. To keep Jason safe, they took him away from the mob and sent everyone home.

Paul found his experience at Thessalonica to be one of his most difficult ones because of the persecution that he and Silas had received. Later, when Timothy brought news from the congregation at Thessalonica, Paul decided to write them a letter. Today, we find that letter in our Bible. It is called First Thessalonians.

In First Thessalonians, Paul writes about the troubles that he heard they were having in their church group. For example, some of the Christians were worried that loved ones who had died since becoming Christians would not be resurrected when Jesus came. Paul reminded the new believers about the importance to our salvation of the death and resurrection of Jesus. He also told them about the existence of Satan and his work to deceive the church. However, it was Paul's teachings about the second coming of Jesus and the future resurrection of the righteous dead that encouraged the church group the most.

The crowd was so angry that they dragged Jason before the rulers of the city.

The messenger who took Paul's first letter to the Thessalonians brought back a report that was not good. Fanatics were making trouble in the church, so Paul decided to write them another letter immediately.

In his second letter to the Thessalonians, he urged those who were weak spiritually to be strong in the Lord. He prayed that they might resist Satan and his troublemakers and live every day for Jesus until He comes.

He also encouraged the Christians to be as humble as Jesus was. They must rejoice in the trials they faced and in the victories they had won for the church in Thessalonica. They must treat one another with brotherly kindness just as Jesus had done. Above all, Paul reminded them of Jesus' promise that He would come again someday soon.

Our Prayer:

"Dear Heavenly Father, help me to be willing to share the story of Jesus anytime I can with whomever will listen."

Hidden Treasure Questions:

✔ How many Sabbaths did Paul and Silas discuss the Scriptures with the believers in Thessalonica?

✔ What are the names of the two books in the Bible that Paul wrote to the Thessalonians?

Listen to this story online!

Scan for bonus content

Who Is the Unknown God?

This story is taken from Acts 17 and *The Acts of the Apostles*, chapter 23.

Paul and Silas had been in Thessalonica for a while, but it wasn't safe for them anymore. So the brothers and sisters in the church sent them away to Berea late one night. When the two missionaries arrived and the Sabbath day rolled around again, they had to make a decision. Should they go to the Jewish synagogue as they usually did? It was the best place to meet with the believers. But would they be treated badly as they had been in Thessalonica?

The Bible tells us that there was a big difference in the character of the people in Berea. Paul and Silas decided to go to the synagogue and found the Jews at Berea to be fair-minded. They were much more reasonable than the Jews in Thessalonica. The Bible says, "They received the word with all readiness, and searched the Scriptures daily to find out whether these things were so" (Acts 17:11). In other words, they didn't take Paul's and Silas' word for anything.

Paul and Silas decided to go to the synagogue and found the Jews at Berea to be fair-minded.

They studied the Scriptures for themselves to see if the good news being preached to them was true. They wanted to learn more about the prophecies that pointed to Jesus the Messiah.

As they studied, they compared the Scriptures verse by verse. Heavenly angels were beside them to open their hearts and impress their minds that they might understand what they were reading. As a result, many of the Jews and Greeks believed, and important women in the city did as well.

Unfortunately, when the Jews from Thessalonica heard about the success that Paul and Silas were having in Berea, trouble started all over again. They were not satisfied to have driven the missionaries from Thessalonica. Soon they arrived and stirred up the crowds in Berea, too.

The enemies of the church could not always prevent the gospel from being preached. However, they could make it very hard for God's people by persecuting them wherever they went. This was Satan's plan, and he hoped to discourage Paul and the others who were working so hard to spread the good news of the gospel.

And yet Paul kept preaching, even under fire. He must not stop preaching because Jesus Himself had asked him to do it so that others might be saved. In his mind, Paul clearly remembered his conversion experience in Damascus, when God had said that he was a chosen vessel to preach Jesus' name before Gentiles, kings, and the children of Israel.

However, wishing to prevent further trouble for Paul in Berea, the new church members there immediately sent him away. Silas and Timothy remained behind to continue the work there, and Paul headed to Athens with instructions that his two missionary partners should come join him as soon as possible.

While Paul waited for Timothy and Silas to arrive, he took a good tour of the city to see where the greatest challenges lay. Athens was a center for architecture, art, and theater. It was one of the most astounding cities in that part of the world.

The Bereans studied the Scriptures for themselves to see if the good news being preached to them was true.

One thing was sure: The city was full of idols and shrines. The worship of pagan gods seemed to be the most important thing to the Athenians. Every garden, temple, and street corner in the city was dedicated to idols.

When the Sabbath day arrived, Paul went to the synagogues in Athens to present the gospel of Jesus, as he usually did, and to reason with both the Jew and Gentile worshippers. And he did more. To reach the people who did not go to the synagogues, he went to the marketplace daily to talk with whomever happened to be there.

Now, Athens was well known for its philosophers. The people were very intelligent and loved to debate old and new ideas. Paul was very educated and an excellent public speaker. When word got out that a new philosopher had come to town, everyone wanted to know who he was. Some called him a babbler, while others said he was bringing the idea of a new foreign god to town. This was because they had heard that he preached about Jesus and the resurrection.

Some of the local philosophers brought Paul to the Areopagus, the most famous meeting place in Athens, where people discussed everything. "May we know what this new doctrine is of which you speak?" they asked him. "You are bringing some strange things to our ears. Therefore, we want to know what these things mean."

Paul stood up in the Areopagus and said, "Men of Athens, I perceive that in all things you are very religious; for as I was passing through and considering the objects of your worship, I even found an altar with this inscription: TO THE UNKNOWN GOD.

"Therefore, the One whom you worship without knowing, Him I proclaim to you. God, who made the world and everything in it, since He is Lord of heaven and earth, does not dwell in temples made with hands. Nor is He worshipped with men's hands, as though He needed anything, since He gives to all life, breath, and all things."

Paul went on to talk about the idols of gold and silver that the people in Athens worshipped, and that God was nothing like them. He was much bigger and more powerful than all this and wanted the Athenians to put away their ideas of worshipping the silly idols. A day was coming when God would judge the world and all people in it. But Jesus had died for their sins to save them, and had risen from the dead to give them a chance for eternal life.

Now, when the philosophers at the Areopagus heard Paul talk about the resurrection of the dead, some of them mocked him. "Whoever heard of such a thing?" we can imagine them scoffing. However, others seemed interested in the philosophy of such an idea. "We will hear you again on this matter," they said.

Unfortunately, there were very few converts in Athens who believed the message that Paul was preaching. Among those who believed, however, were Dionysius, who was a philosopher at the Areopagite, and a woman named Damaris.

Paul stood up in the Areopagus and said, "Men of Athens, I perceive that in all things you are very religious."

It is not likely that Paul went back to the Areopagus anytime soon. The philosophers were not looking for a Savior. They just wanted to discuss ideas and debate them with one another.

But the Bible and the messages went out to that city nevertheless. We, as Christians, are to tell everyone we can about Jesus and His soon return. We are not responsible for the way people react to God's Word. We are to be a light to the world, so whether we are old or young, we should let our light shine.

"Dear Father in heaven, I need to be able to share the gospel with everyone: the rich and the poor, the educated and those who don't have much education. Help me to do it as Jesus would."

Hidden Treasure Questions:

✔ How were the Jews in Berea different from the Jews in Thessalonica?

✔ What unusual thing did Paul notice about the city of Athens?

Listen to this story online!

Scan for bonus content

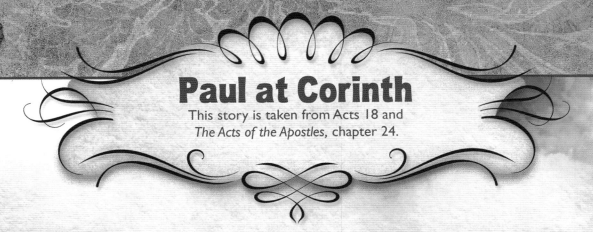

Paul at Corinth

This story is taken from Acts 18 and
The Acts of the Apostles, chapter 24.

Paul moved on from Athens without much success. He was such a godly man and a very good speaker, so he was not used to a failure of this kind. However, he did learn some lessons from his time there. From now on when he preached, he was going to preach only about Jesus' death and resurrection as the hope of every Christian.

Next, he went to Corinth, and there he stayed with a Jew named Aquila, who had recently come there from Italy. He and his wife, Priscilla, had settled in Corinth after Emperor Claudius had commanded that all Jews must leave Rome.

It was a perfect place for Paul to stay because he was of the same trade as Aquila and Priscilla. They all worked together at making tents. Although Paul was a very educated man, as all good Jews in those days, he had learned the skills of a trade as a boy.

Corinth was a perfect place for Paul to stay because he was of the same trade as Aquila and Priscilla.

The city of Corinth was a leading city in that part of the world. It was the home of Greeks, Jews, and Romans, with travelers coming through all the time. Corinth was a city of business and pleasure, but it was also one of the most wicked cities of its day. Idol worship was a big part of the Corinthian way of life. Venus was their most famous goddess, and the things people did while worshipping her were shameful. Even among the people who were not Christians or Jews, the city was considered a very bad place where people lived only for themselves.

On the Sabbath day, Paul went to the synagogue with Aquila and Priscilla, as was his custom. While there, he preached to the Jews and taught them that Jesus Christ was the Son of God. This made the Jewish worshippers angry, and they argued with him about it.

When Paul realized that they would not accept his message, he finally shook off his garments, as was the symbolic custom in his day. "Your blood be upon your own heads!" he told them. "I am clean. From now on, I will go to the Gentiles."

Since Paul's earliest days as a Christian, it had been his goal to persuade Jews that Jesus was the Messiah and the Savior of the world. But now he could see that Jews everywhere did not want to hear the gospel and were rejecting it.

After he went to the synagogue that day, Paul went to the home of Justus. This man was a godly influence in the community, and his house was next door to the synagogue.

Paul was a bit discouraged after his rejection at the Jewish synagogue. However, he did feel good about the few who believed in his message of salvation. Crispus, the ruler of the synagogue, was one of them. He and his entire household accepted Jesus as their Savior and were baptized.

One night, the Lord spoke to Paul in a vision: "Do not be afraid, but speak, and do not keep silent; for I am with you. No one will attack you to hurt you; for I have many people in this city."

As the weeks and months passed, Paul

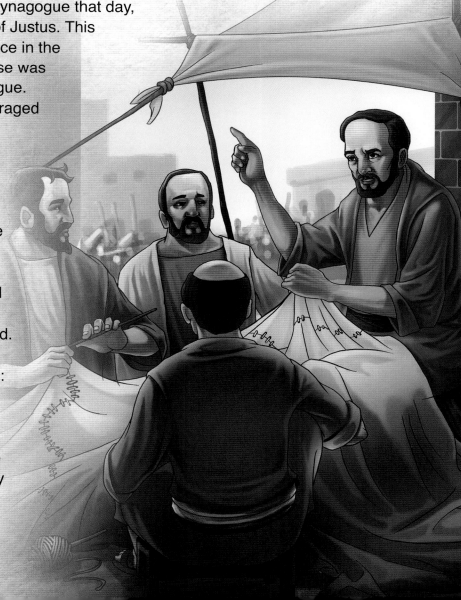

found these words to be true and continued to teach those who would listen. Many of the Corinthians who had heard him preach also believed and were baptized. So Paul stayed in Corinth for a year and a half teaching the word of God among the Corinthian believers.

When he left Corinth to work in Achaia, the Jews made trouble for him there, too.

One night, the Lord spoke to Paul in a vision: "Do not be afraid, but speak, and do not keep silent."

They banded together and took Paul before the judgment seat of Gallio, the proconsul of Achaia. "This fellow persuades men to worship God contrary to the law!" they said.

Paul was ready to defend himself before the proconsul, but Gallio held up his hand. "If it were a matter of wrongdoing or wicked crimes, there would be reason why I should bear with you," he said to the Jews. "But if it is a question of words and names and your own law, look to it yourselves, for I do not want to be a judge of such matters." That was the end of the matter, and Gallio ordered them to leave his court.

Now the tables were turned because the Greeks at the court could see what kind of people the Jews in Corinth actually were. They were not a peace-loving people, but enjoyed making trouble for good people like Paul.

In a fit of rage, the Greeks took Sosthenes, the ruler of the synagogue who had brought Paul to court, and beat him outside in the street. Gallio knew what was happening, but he did nothing to rescue Sosthenes.

"Dear Jesus, it can be discouraging sharing the gospel with people who don't want to hear it, but help me to remember that people rejected You, too."

Hidden Treasure Questions:

✔ What was the difference in the way Paul preached in Athens and Corinth?

✔ What was the name of the Roman proconsul who refused to hear complaints from the Jews against Paul?

Listen to this story online!

Scan for bonus content

Healed by a Handkerchief

This story is taken from Acts 19 and
The Acts of the Apostles, chapters 26 and 27.

Paul had been traveling as a missionary evangelist for many years now. The Lord had been with him to lead and protect him as he spread the gospel to every city, province, and country. He had been through much since his conversion experience on the road to Damascus.

One day he was being worshipped as a god, and the next he was being stoned. One hour he was casting out demons, and the next he was being thrown into prison.

About this time, Paul arrived in Ephesus, a very famous city in what we now call the country of Turkey. Ephesus was a city of business and culture. Everyone wanted to live there, and people from all over the world came to trade in its ports.

As was his custom when he first came to town, Paul usually went to a local synagogue to preach and teach the Word of God. For three months, he spoke boldly, "reasoning and persuading the people concerning the things of the Kingdom of God."

Paul met all kinds of people as he spread the good news of salvation. In Ephesus, he found 12 men who were followers of Apollos. Apollos was a talented evangelist who was working for God in Corinth. "Did you receive the Holy Spirit when you first believed?" Paul asked them.

They looked at Paul in surprise and replied, "We have not so much as heard whether there is a Holy Spirit."

Then it was Paul's turn to be surprised. "Into what then were you baptized?" he asked.

"Into John's baptism."

Then Paul said, "John indeed baptized with a baptism of repentance, saying to the people that they should believe on Him who would come after him, that is, on Christ Jesus."

The 12 men accepted the good news of the gospel, and then they were baptized in the name of Jesus. Paul afterward laid his hands on them, and they were suddenly filled with the Holy Spirit. With new power in their lives, they received the ability to speak in foreign tongues and prophesy.

The 12 men accepted the good news of the gospel, and then they were baptized in the name of Jesus. Paul afterward laid his hands on them.

But not everyone in those synagogue meetings was as open to the things that Paul was preaching. Some resisted the power of the Holy Spirit and hardened their heart to the message. They did not believe and spoke evil of the "Way," which was another name for the new Christian movement of the early church.

Because they opposed Paul and wanted to argue with him, Paul stopped coming to their meetings. Instead, he started meeting with the Christian believers in the school of Tyrannus. There he met with them every day, studying and reasoning from the Scriptures.

For two years Paul continued training the young men and women to share the word of God. As these workers took the message back to their cities and provinces, the gospel spread quickly. Soon it seemed that everyone in Asia had heard the teaching of the Lord Jesus, both Jews and Greeks.

Paul began doing miracles of healing in Ephesus. People came from everywhere to be healed by him. Many went home praising God for these demonstrations of heaven's power. In some cases, those who could not reach Paul were given handkerchiefs or aprons that had been touched by him. When these were sent back to the sick people, they were healed.

But it was Paul's healings of the demoniacs that were often the most dramatic. When he spoke in Jesus' name, the evil spirits had to leave, though they sometimes came out with great difficulty. The word spread that Paul was casting out demons, and the people had the opportunity to see that the God of heaven was more powerful than the magicians. Among the Jews, there were many who used sorcery to work magic, and they wanted to be able to do wonders just as Paul did.

Seven sons of a priest named Sceva tried casting out a demon in Jesus' name, just as Paul had done.

Seven sons of a priest named Sceva tried casting out a demon in Jesus' name, just as Paul had done, but it was a disaster. "In the name of the Jesus whom Paul preaches, we command you to come out!" they said.

But the demon in the man did not think highly of the seven men, and he let them know it. "Jesus I know, and Paul I know," he growled, "but who are you?" Then he chased the men, leaped upon them, and overpowered them. The men were so frightened that they ran out of the man's house naked and wounded.

The story of these seven men and their battle with Satan became public news to everyone all over Ephesus. And so the fear of God came upon everyone, and the name of Jesus was glorified.

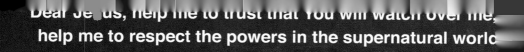

Dear Jesus, help me to trust that You will watch over me,
help me to respect the powers in the supernatural world

Hidden Treasure Questions:

✔ What unusual things did Paul sometimes
do to heal people?

✔ How many sons did Sceva have
who learned not to use Jesus'
name carelessly?

Listen to this story online!

Scan for bonus content

Success and Danger in Ephesus

This story is taken from Acts 19 and
The Acts of the Apostles, chapter 27.

Paul had been in Ephesus for almost two years now and was having real success in bringing people to Jesus. Not only did he preach in the synagogues, but he also taught classes every day. There they studied the Scriptures and trained workers to be missionaries.

But one of the most amazing things that he did in Ephesus, through the power of God, was the miraculous healing of those who were sick and demon-possessed.

Because of this, the believers had a new respect for God, and for Paul, who was His messenger. Many of them had practiced magic and regularly visited fortune-tellers, but that began to change. In many cases, the pagan sorcerers themselves even believed in the power of God over Satan. There was such a change in their hearts that they brought their books and scrolls on magic to be burned in a big bonfire in the streets of Ephesus. When they counted up the value of the books, it totaled almost 50,000 pieces of silver.

This burning of the books showed that the Ephesian believers had given up their old way of life. The books had been one of Satan's strongest doors to their hearts, but once they had given the books up, he had no more power over them. The things they had once loved so much they now hated, and that is exactly what happens when Jesus comes into someone's life.

The Ephesians brought their books and scrolls on magic to be burned in a big bonfire in the streets of Ephesus.

Others continued to close their hearts to the good news of the gospel that Paul was bringing them. They saw Christianity as trouble because they did not want to give up their pagan way of life. Ephesus was full of idols to all kinds of gods and goddesses.

These pagan gods supposedly required their worshippers to do many evil things that Christians should never do.

Paul's message to the people of Ephesus was that worshipping idols was wrong. Jesus Christ was the Creator of all things. He was the one true God, and the only One worthy of their worship.

Some in Ephesus began to think about the problems that this might cause in the worship of the gods and goddesses at the local temples. If people were being told that they should worship only Jesus, the Son of God, there would be fewer people going to the temples to worship.

Demetrius, one of the local silversmiths, was one of the first to realize this, and he wasn't too happy about it. He made silver idols to Diana, who

The silversmiths and shop owners got angry as they listened to Demetrius. "Great is Diana of the Ephesians!" they began to shout.

happened to be the most important goddess of the Ephesians. Because everyone worshipped her in the city of Ephesus, the sale of these idols brought in a lot of money to the craftsmen who made them.

But all that would change now if the Christians were allowed to stay in Ephesus. As far as Demetrius was concerned, the new preachers in town were to blame, and especially Paul.

And sure enough, the number of idols being sold at the shops along the streets began to drop. Demetrius sent out messengers to call in all the silversmiths and shop owners to talk about what they should do. "Men, you know that we have our prosperity by this trade," he said. "Moreover, you see and hear that not only at Ephesus, but throughout almost all Asia, this Paul has persuaded and turned away many people, saying that our idols are not really gods. So not only is this trade of ours in danger, but also the temple of the great goddess Diana may be despised and her magnificence destroyed, whom all Asia and the world worship."

The silversmiths and shop owners got angry as they listened to Demetrius. He was right, and they knew they had to do something about it. "Great is Diana of the Ephesians!" they began to shout, and soon their anger spread to the streets. Before long the commotion was everywhere as people took up the chant, "Great is Diana of the Ephesians!"

The crowd became a mob and began running through the streets until they found Gaius and Aristarchus, two of Paul's traveling companions from Macedonia. Grabbing the two men, they rushed with them into the public theater as they continued shouting, "Great is Diana of the Ephesians! Great is Diana of the Ephesians!"

Most of the people in the mob did not know what the commotion was all about, or why everyone had come to the theater. They had heard the crowds shouting and seen the people running, and they joined in because of all the excitement.

When Paul heard the deafening noise of the crowds coming from the theater, he was worried. When they told him that Gaius and Aristarchus had been taken there by the mob, he was frightened for their safety. He wanted to go to the theater immediately to calm down the crowds, but his friends begged him not to go near the place.

The crowds were getting angrier by the minute because they couldn't find Paul. Now other Jews in the crowd began to get worried. If they weren't careful, things might turn out badly for all the Jews because of him. So they urged Alexander, a fellow Jew, to explain that they had nothing to do with Paul. However, when the crowds discovered that Alexander was a Jew, they got angry and cried out, "Great is Diana of the Ephesians!"

The mob kept this up for two hours until the city clerk arrived. He finally got the crowds to quiet down enough to talk to them. "Men of Ephesus," he said, "what man is there who does not know that the city of the Ephesians is temple guardian of the great goddess Diana, and of the image which fell down from Zeus?

"Therefore, since these things cannot be denied, you ought to be quiet and do nothing rashly. For you have brought these men here who are neither robbers of temples nor blasphemers of your goddess. Therefore, if Demetrius and his fellow craftsmen have a case against anyone, the courts are open and there are proconsuls. Let them bring charges against each other."

The city clerk was not pleased with everyone in the mob for the disturbance that they were causing. Unless they wanted more trouble, his advice was that they should all go home. And that is exactly what they did. Within minutes the crowds had dispersed and the streets cleared.

And so it was that God protected Paul once again from the dangers at the hands of evil men. The apostle had a job to do for God, and nothing in this world could keep him from doing it. Satan would have loved to destroy Paul, but the angels from heaven kept him safe.

The mob kept shouting for two hours until the city clerk arrived. He finally got the crowds to quiet down enough to talk to them.

Our Prayer:

"Dear God, thank You that I am free from magic and the worship of idols. Please keep me safe from such things."

Hidden Treasure Questions:

✔ How much were the magic books worth that were burned in the streets of Ephesus?

✔ What was the name of the famous goddess of the Ephesians?

Listen to this story online!

Scan for bonus content

A Young Man Falls to His Death

This story is taken from Acts 20 and
The Acts of the Apostles, chapter 37.

After the riot in Ephesus, the church leaders felt that it would be safer for Paul if they got him out of town. So Paul called all of the believers together for one last meeting and encouraged them to be faithful to Jesus. Then with many tears and hugs, they sent him off to Macedonia. When he arrived in Greece, he preached the word of God for about three months to the Jews and Gentiles alike in the local Jewish synagogue. However, once again, the Jews got angry because they didn't agree with his message that Jesus Christ was the Messiah and the Son of God.

At the end of the three months, Paul decided he would have to leave Greece. However, as he was getting ready to sail to Syria, he heard that the Jews were plotting to kill him. Therefore, he changed his plans and decided to return by land through Macedonia.

This time he had several companions go with him who had joined him from cities along the way. These disciples were from Berea, Thessalonica, Derbe, and Asia. When they reached Troas, they stayed there for seven days.

On the first day of the week, everyone came together to break bread and meet with Paul. There must have been quite a reunion of believers who had come to love Paul and the gospel he preached. Paul was such an interesting speaker, and since he was going to leave the next day, everyone stayed very late at the church to hear his words.

All evening, he told them stories about the good things that God was doing among the Gentiles. He probably told the story about the night that they spent at the jail in Philippi, how the earthquake had opened the prison doors, and how the jailer was baptized because of it all. He probably shared the story about the seven sons of Sceva who had tried to cast demons out in Jesus' name, but had then been beaten themselves. Then, of course, there was the story of how the Christians in Ephesus had burned their books about magic and witchcraft.

Sitting on the windowsill of the room was a young man named Eutychus who kept nodding off as Paul preached.

One story led to another, and before everyone knew it, the hour was very late. The time was well past midnight, and everyone was getting tired. There were many lamps in the upper room where they were meeting, and that probably made the room warm and stuffy.

Sitting on the windowsill of the room was a young man named Eutychus who kept nodding off as Paul preached. He got so sleepy that he finally dropped into a deep sleep and fell out the window. Unfortunately, the room where they were meeting was three stories up.

In shock and horror, everybody ran down to the street to find that Eutychus was already dead. There he lay in the street, his body crumpled and broken. What a

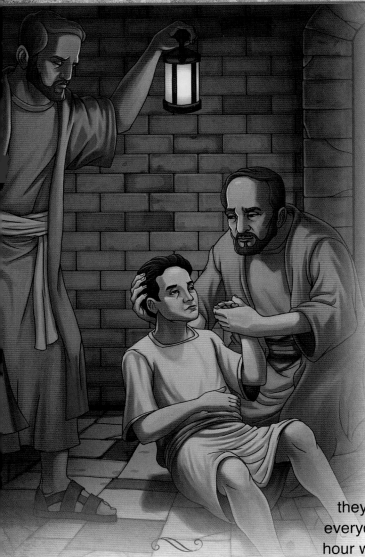

terrible tragedy! the church members must have thought. They had wanted one last meeting with Paul before he left, but now Satan had struck again and ruined their happiness.

The evil one might have enjoyed the few moments of pain and suffering he could cause the church group at Troas, but God can bring joy out of pain. When Paul saw the young man, he bent down and hugged him. Then he said to the people standing around crying, "Do not trouble yourselves, for his life is in him."

And it was so! Eutychus was raised to life. This was a mighty miracle from God. No one could fall three stories to a hard stone street and live to tell about it. But God is good and had given Paul the power to raise the boy to life again.

What rejoicing there was when they all realized what had happened. Now everyone was wide-awake. Though the hour was late, they all went upstairs again, retelling the events of the night. And they broke bread again, ate a meal together, and talked some more about how God had blessed them.

By now, it was morning. As the dawn broke, Paul said goodbye and left for the next stop on his journey.

When Paul saw the young man, he bent down and hugged him. Eutychus was raised to life.

Our Prayer:

"Dear Jesus, help me to be faithful in attending the prayer meetings in my local church."

Hidden Treasure Questions:

✓ How late did Paul preach on his last night in Troas?

✓ What was the name of the young man who fell asleep sitting on the windowsill, fell to the street, and was raised to life again by Paul?

Listen to this story online!

Scan for bonus content

Saved by the Romans

This story is taken from Acts 21 and 22 and
The Acts of the Apostles, chapters 37 and 38.

Paul wanted to go to Rome to preach the gospel, but first he felt he needed to go to Jerusalem one last time. People kept telling him that it was too dangerous, because they knew that there were people in Judea who wanted to see him dead.

Along the way, as they stopped in seaport cities, he met and worshipped with the believers. People were so glad to see him, but they were worried, too. Women and children would come out with their husbands to pray and ask God to give Paul a safe journey.

In Caesarea, Paul and his companions stayed with Philip, the evangelist. While he was there, many people came to see him, including a prophet named Agabus from Judea. Like many others, he told Paul not to go to Jerusalem because it wasn't safe. To make his point, he took Paul's belt and tied up his own hands and feet with it.

Agabus then said, "Thus says the Holy Spirit, so shall the Jews at Jerusalem bind the man who owns this belt, and deliver him into the hands of the Gentiles."

The officer then took Paul and ordered his soldiers to bind Paul with two chains. He thought that Paul must be a dangerous criminal.

Now others pleaded with him not to go to Jerusalem, but Paul ignored their fears. Then Paul said, "What do you mean by weeping and breaking my heart? For I am ready not only to be bound, but also to die at Jerusalem for the name of the Lord Jesus."

Everyone could see that it was no use trying to convince him to stay, so they stopped trying and said, "The will of the Lord be done."

When the traveling party arrived in Jerusalem, the church members and leaders were happy to see him. The next day James and all of the church elders called a meeting, and Paul shared the testimony of what God was doing among the Gentiles through his ministry.

Everyone praised the Lord when they heard Paul's stories of how God was working among both the Jews and Gentiles. However, they warned him that some of the Jewish believers had started rumors that Paul was teaching Jews to disobey the laws of Moses. They knew that this wasn't true, so they urged him to rededicate himself at the temple by taking a vow for seven days.

Paul agreed to do this, but it seemed to do little good. At the end of the seven days, some troublemaking Jews from Asia saw him in the temple and stirred up a crowd of people. "Men of Israel, help! This is the man who teaches all men everywhere against the people, the law, and this place. Furthermore, he also brought Greeks into the temple and has defiled this holy place."

Agabus told Paul not to go to Jerusalem. To make his point, he took Paul's belt and tied up his own hands and feet with it.

This wasn't true, of course. Paul loved his people and the temple. But the visiting Jews jumped to that conclusion because they had seen Trophimus, a Greek church member from Ephesus, with him in the city.

By now it seemed that the whole city of Jerusalem was turning into a riot. The mob found Paul, grabbed him, and dragged him out of the temple, intending to kill him. News of this reached Lysias, the Roman commander of the garrison, so he immediately took his centurions and soldiers and ran into the crowds to stop the riot.

Fortunately, when the crowd saw the commander and the soldiers, they stopped beating Paul. The officer then took him and ordered his soldiers to bind Paul with two chains. He thought that Paul must be a dangerous criminal or the crowd wouldn't be so violent.

"Who are you? What have you done?" he asked Paul, but the noise of the riot was so loud that he couldn't hear what the apostle was saying.

"Away with him!" the crowd kept shouting. "Away with him!"

Finally, Lysias ordered that Paul be taken inside the barracks so he could find out the truth about him. However, when they reached the Roman garrison, the crowd was so violent that Paul had to be carried up the stairs.

When they reached the top of the stairs going into the barracks, Paul asked the commander, "May I speak to you?"

"Can you speak Greek?" Lysias asked. "Are you not the Egyptian who started a rebellion some time ago and led 4,000 assassins out into the wilderness?"

"I am a Jew from Tarsus, in Cilicia, a very important city," replied Paul. "I beg of you, please allow me to speak to the people."

The commander must have been surprised that Paul would ask for such a thing, but he gave him permission to speak. Then Paul motioned with his hands for the crowds to be quiet and spoke to them in the Hebrew language.

He told them how he had grown up as a Jew and sat at the feet of the great teacher Gamaliel. He told the crowds that he had been very zealous toward God and had persecuted Christians, even putting some to death, such as Stephen. He shared his conversion experience on the road to Damascus, telling how he had been healed of blindness by Ananias and then was baptized. He told about his escape in a basket over the wall of Damascus, only to be threatened with death again when he reached Jerusalem.

"But the Lord had plans for me and told me to leave Jerusalem," Paul said. "He told me that He wanted to send me far from here to the Gentiles."

The crowd seemed interested in what Paul was saying until he reached the part about preaching to the Gentiles, instead of the Jews.

"Away with such a fellow from the earth," they shouted again, "for he is not fit to live!" Then they tore their clothes and tossed dust into the air, as was the custom in those days for people who wanted to show great anger or sorrow.

Finally, the crowd got so loud and angry again that Lysias ordered that Paul be taken inside the barracks. Then he told his soldiers to scourge him and ask him questions to find out why the crowds were so angry with him.

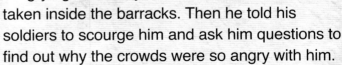

The crowd got so loud and angry again that Lysias ordered that Paul be taken inside the barracks.

As the soldiers were tying his hands, Paul asked a centurion who was standing nearby, "Is it lawful for you to scourge a man who is a Roman and not condemned?"

The centurion was shocked when he heard this and went to the commander. "Take care what you do, for this man is a Roman," he said.

Lysias was worried now too. "Tell me, are you a Roman?" he asked in disbelief. "Yes," Paul replied.

"With a large sum, I obtained this citizenship," the commander said proudly.

And Paul said, "But I was born a citizen."

And so it was that those who were going to chastise Paul backed off and released him, because they realized that they were about to beat a Roman citizen illegally.

Our Prayer:

"Dear Father in heaven, help me to be willing to speak for You anytime, anywhere, as Paul did."

Hidden Treasure Questions:

✔ What prophet warned Paul not to go down to Jerusalem?

✔ Why was the crowd so angry with Paul?

Listen to this story online!

Scan for bonus content

Paul Before the Sanhedrin

This story is taken from Acts 23 and
The Acts of the Apostles, chapter 38.

The Roman commander Lysias wanted to keep peace in Jerusalem. The Jews there hated Paul. They wanted to see him dead because of crimes that they said he had done in their temple. But Lysias was sure that Paul was innocent, and decided to have him brought to trial before the Jewish Sanhedrin just in case.

The next day, he ordered the chief priests and elders of the Jewish council to meet together and question Paul. The apostle knew that this was probably his last chance to speak to all of the Jewish leaders like this, and he felt sure that God had arranged it. Maybe with God's help, he could say the right words to help some of them accept Jesus as their Savior.

"Men and brethren, I have lived with a clear conscience before God until this day," he began as the trial started. But that was as far as he got because the high priest, Ananias, ordered someone standing nearby to slap him on the face.

Paul was not happy to be treated this way, and he told Ananias what he thought. "God will strike you, you whitewashed wall! For you sit to judge me according to the law, and yet you command that someone hit me, which is against the law!"

> Lysias was sure that Paul was innocent, and decided to have him brought to trial before the Jewish Sanhedrin just in case.

"Do you criticize God's high priest?" someone demanded.

Paul did not know that he was the high priest, because he now apologized for speaking to him in that tone of voice. However, by the way they were treating him, he realized that this trial was already going nowhere. All it would take now to end this meeting was a little controversy between the Sadducees and Pharisees who sat on the council.

And that is exactly what Paul did. He started an argument between the two groups by saying, "Men and brethren, I am a Pharisee, the son of a Pharisee. I am being judged because of my hope in the resurrection of the dead!"

At this comment, everyone suddenly forgot that Paul was the one on trial because the council was divided. Sadducees did not believe in a resurrection, or angels, or spirits. Pharisees believed in all three.

By now everyone was shouting at one another. Some of the scribes among the Pharisees said, "We find no evil in this man. If a spirit or an angel has spoken to him, let us not fight against God."

Then the place turned into a madhouse. Some were trying to reach Paul to beat him, while others tried to protect him. The Roman commander was afraid that Paul was going to be torn to pieces, so he ordered his soldiers to go down to the Sanhedrin floor and bring him back to the barracks.

This was really sad. As with Jesus at His crucifixion trial, Paul was actually safer among the Romans than he was with his own people.

But Paul didn't need to worry. God was with him every step of the way. The following night Jesus came to see him and said, "Be of good cheer, Paul; for as you have testified for Me in Jerusalem, so you must also bear witness at Rome."

And God's message came none too soon. At this time, a group of 40 Jews banded together to plot the death of Paul. In fact, they went to the chief priests and elders and told them, "We have bound ourselves under a great oath that we will eat nothing until we have killed Paul."

Then they suggested that the Jewish council ask the Roman commander to bring Paul down to the Sanhedrin one more time for questioning. Of course, that was not the real plan. On the way to the hearing, they intended to attack and kill him.

Paul's nephew somehow heard about the planned ambush and went to the barracks to tell Paul about it.

However, Paul's nephew somehow heard about the planned ambush and went to the barracks to tell Paul about it. Paul then called for one of the centurions and told him, "Take this young man to the commander, for he has something to tell him."

So the centurion took Paul's nephew to Lysias, who pulled the boy aside privately.

"The Jews have agreed to ask that you bring Paul down to the council tomorrow as though they were going to ask more questions," said Paul's nephew. "But don't listen to them, because more than 40 of them are laying an ambush for him. These men have bound themselves by an oath to kill Paul while he is on his way to the trial."

Lysias was impressed with the boy's bravery at bringing such a message. "Tell no one that you have revealed these things to me," he said. And with that, he made a plan to send Paul away by night guarded by a small army of soldiers and horsemen.

Our Prayer:

"Dear Heavenly Father, I want to be a strong witness for You, even if people don't treat me well."

Hidden Treasure Questions:

✔ What was the name of the Roman commander in charge of keeping Paul safe?

✔ What did Paul say that started the Sadducees and Pharisees fighting in the Jewish council?

Listen to this story online!

Scan for bonus content

A King Almost Becomes a Christian

This story is taken from Acts 23-26 and
The Acts of the Apostles, chapters 39 and 40.

Paul's life was in danger, and there wasn't a minute to spare. His nephew had warned him that a band of 40 Jews had taken a vow to kill him, and when the Roman commander Lysias found out, he came up with a plan.

Immediately he called for two centurions. "Prepare 200 soldiers, 70 horsemen, and 200 spearmen to go to Caesarea at the third hour of the night," (9:00 p.m.) he told them. "And provide mounts to set Paul on and take him safely to Felix, the governor."

Then he wrote a letter to the governor and told him, "This man was seized by the Jews and was about to be killed by them. Coming with the troops, I rescued him, having learned that he was a Roman. When I wanted to know the reason that they accused him, I brought him before their council. I found out that he was accused concerning questions of their law, but had nothing charged against him deserving of death or chains. When it was told me that the Jews lay in wait for the man, I sent him immediately to you. I also commanded his accusers to state before you the charges against him."

Then the soldiers, as they were commanded, took Paul by night to the city of Antipatris. The next day the horsemen went on ahead to take Paul to Caesarea, along with the letter from Lysias to the governor.

When the governor met Paul, he put him in Herod's Praetorium. There Paul waited until the trial, when his Jewish accusers should come down from Jerusalem.

Five days later, the high priest, Ananias, arrived with a famous speaker named Tertullus and a group of elders. Tertullus accused

Paul of being a troublemaker among the Jews in Jerusalem. He claimed that Paul had tried to defile the temple, but that the Roman commander Lysias took him away by force.

Then Paul was given a chance to speak and defend himself. "It has been only 12 days since I went up to Jerusalem to worship. They never saw me arguing in the temple with anyone, or stirring up the crowds," said Paul. "The only thing I said that made them angry was that I believe there will be a resurrection of the dead, and for that I am being judged by you this day."

When Felix heard Paul's explanation about why he was on trial, he put the trial on hold. "When Lysias the commander comes down, I will make a decision on your case," he told Paul. Then he ordered the centurion to put Paul under house arrest and told him

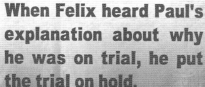

When Felix heard Paul's explanation about why he was on trial, he put the trial on hold.

Agrippa nodded slowly as he looked at Paul. "You almost persuade me to become a Christian," he said.

that Paul would be allowed to have friends visit him.

Then some time later, Felix sent for Paul again. He and his wife, Drusilla, who was a Jew, wanted to hear Paul talk about his faith in Christ. As Paul talked about spiritual things such as righteousness and the coming judgment, Felix became afraid.

"Go away for now; and when I have a convenient time, I will call for you," he told Paul. From time to time, he would send for Paul so that they could talk, but secretly he was hoping that Paul would give him money for his freedom.

This went on for two years until Porcius Festus became governor instead of Felix. Three days after Festus came to power, he went up from Caesarea to Jerusalem. The Jewish leaders then met with him and asked him about Paul, requesting that Paul be brought up to Jerusalem. However, they planned to set an ambush along the way to kill him.

But Festus told them that Paul would be kept at Caesarea. If they wanted to discuss his case further to find any fault in him, they should come down to Caesarea again.

When Festus went back down to Caesarea 10 days later, the Jewish leaders went with him. When Festus was on his judgment seat, he called for Paul. The Jews again made some serious complaints that they could not prove, and Paul defended himself.

"Neither against the law of the Jews, nor against the temple, nor against Caesar have I done anything wrong," he said.

However, like Felix, Festus wanted to please the Jews. Therefore, he asked Paul, "Are you willing to go up to Jerusalem, and there be judged before me concerning these things?"

But Paul knew this was a trick on the part of the Jews, and he wouldn't agree. "I stand at Caesar's judgment seat, where I ought to be judged," he replied. "To the Jews, I have done no wrong, as you very well know. If there is nothing in these things of which these men accuse me, no one can deliver me to them. I appeal to Caesar."

Felix realized that Paul's case was now out of his hands. After speaking to his advisers, he told Paul, "You have appealed to Caesar? To Caesar you shall go!"

Some time later, King Agrippa and his wife, Bernice, came to Caesarea to visit with Festus. After several days, Festus told King Agrippa about Paul and invited him to hear his case.

The next day, Agrippa and Bernice came with the important men of the city. With great fanfare and pomp, they all entered the auditorium.

Paul was then brought in and given a chance to speak on his own behalf. He told of his early upbringing. He told how he had become a Pharisee and persecuted the Christians, shutting up many of them in prison and even executing some. He told how he went to cities outside of Judea to find Christians and was on his way to Damascus when he met Jesus, the Son of God, in vision. That is when Jesus told Paul that He wanted him to go as a missionary to both Jews and Gentiles.

Paul said, "Therefore, King Agrippa, I was not disobedient to the heavenly vision, but declared first to those in Damascus and in Jerusalem, and throughout all the region of Judea, and then to the Gentiles, that they should repent and turn to God. For these reasons, the Jews seized me in the temple and tried to kill me."

Festus grew impatient with Paul at this time and began to mock him. "Much learning is driving you mad!" he said.

Paul was sent away, and with him went King Agrippa's opportunity for salvation.

But again Paul defended himself. "I am not mad, most noble Festus, but speak the words of truth and reason. The king, before whom I also speak freely, knows these things. For I am convinced that none of these things escapes his attention since this thing was not done in secret." Then, turning to King Agrippa, he said, "Do you believe the prophets? I know that you do believe."

Agrippa nodded slowly as he looked at Paul. "You almost persuade me to become a Christian," he said.

Then the hearing was over. Paul was sent away, and with him went King Agrippa's opportunity for salvation. He came close to eternal life that day, but unwisely let the moment pass him by.

Our Prayer:

"Dear God, help me to listen to the voice of the Holy Spirit when You offer me salvation."

Hidden Treasure Questions:

✔ What does it mean to be under house arrest?

✔ What were the names of the three Roman rulers who listened to Paul preach in the royal court of Caesarea?

Listen to this story online!

Scan for bonus content

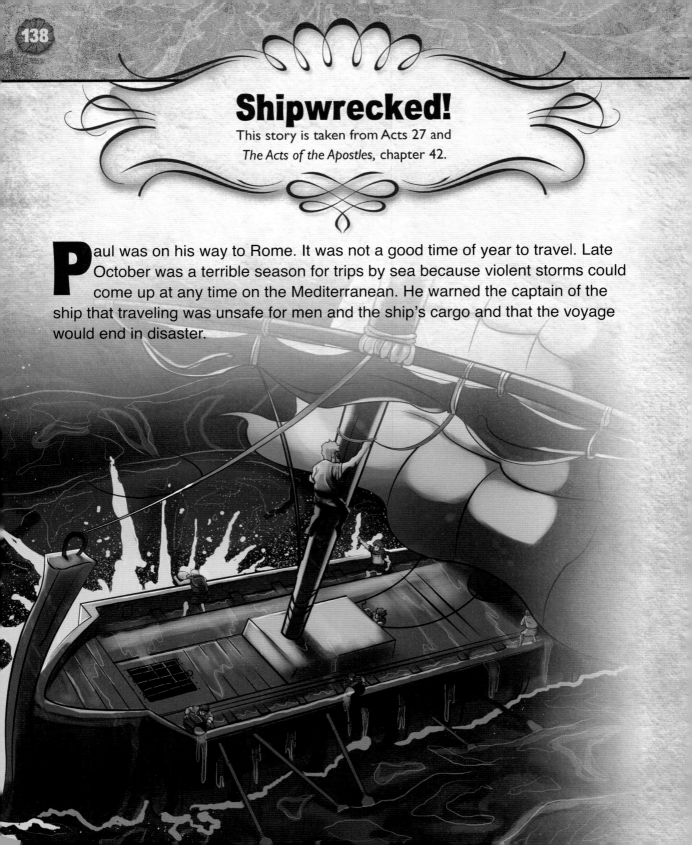

Shipwrecked!

This story is taken from Acts 27 and
The Acts of the Apostles, chapter 42.

Paul was on his way to Rome. It was not a good time of year to travel. Late October was a terrible season for trips by sea because violent storms could come up at any time on the Mediterranean. He warned the captain of the ship that traveling was unsafe for men and the ship's cargo and that the voyage would end in disaster.

But the Roman centurion who was transporting Paul to Rome wouldn't listen. Within a few hours of leaving port, a hurricane called a northeaster swept down off the island. The ship was caught in the storm, and though the sailors tried to turn it into the wind, they were driven off course and finally had to let the ship go with the wind.

Things looked grim. The lifeboat was pulled up on deck to keep it from being beaten to pieces. The storm was so violent that the sailors were worried the ship might come apart.

The captain and his crew thought that they were doomed. Because of the raging storm they could not see the sky to navigate by the sun, moon, or stars, and so they gave up all hope of surviving the storm.

After many days, Paul called the passengers and ship's crew together to give them words of comfort. "God has not abandoned us," he told them. "If you had followed my advice about traveling this late in the season, you would have spared yourself all this damage and loss. However, the most important thing we need to do now is to keep up our courage. All is not lost. Last night an angel of God came to encourage me.

"The angel told me that our ship will run aground on some island and break into pieces, but not one of us will lose our life in this storm. He told me that my work is not yet done. I must stand trial before Caesar, and God will see that I get to Rome."

"So I advise you to keep your spirits up, men, for I have faith in God that everything will happen just as the angel told me."

Paul's angel was right, because in a few days they could hear the surf pounding and guessed that we must be nearing land, so they dropped four anchors from the stern and waited for daylight.

A hurricane called a northeaster swept down off the island. The ship was caught in the storm.

The night passed slowly, and everyone was worried about what would come with the breaking of day. Would the ship take on too much water and sink? Would it run against the rocks along the shoreline and be pounded into splinters? Would everyone drown in the sea? Most couldn't swim, and that worried everyone even more.

Just before dawn, Paul gathered everyone together on deck. "You all need to eat something," he shouted above the pounding of the surf. "For two weeks you have been sick with worry about whether or not we would make it, and you haven't eaten much of anything. Well, today's the day! Don't worry," he reminded them. "Not one of you will lose a single hair from his head."

So Paul took some bread and gave thanks to God for their protection thus far. Then he broke it and passed it around. Everyone was encouraged by Paul's words, and they all ate together.

Paul called the passengers and ship's crew together to give them words of comfort. "God has not abandoned us," he told them.

Daylight had come by now. They could all see the shoreline not far off, but no one recognized the place where they were. When they spotted a sandy beach among the rocks, they decided to steer the ship in that direction and run it aground.

Unfortunately, before they had gone very far the ship struck a sandbar. The bow of the ship stuck there, but the surf pounding the ship from behind began to break the stern into pieces.

There was no time left to think about what to do. Suddenly the ship gave a mighty lurch, and everyone began jumping into the sea. Those who could swim made their way to land, and the rest rode on planks or other pieces of the ship floating in the water.

Amazingly, everyone managed to make it to shore. There were 276 people on board the ship, and not one perished. God had saved them all just as Paul had said He would.

Our Prayer:

"Thank You, Lord, for protecting me from dangers on every side. I know that You have something special for me to do. Help me to be as faithful as Paul."

Hidden Treasure Questions:

✔ How would you feel if you were in a storm at sea?

✔ Paul was saved from a shipwreck so that he could go to the court of Caesar and witness for Jesus. Are you willing to be as brave as Paul was and stand for Jesus no matter how bad things get?

Listen to this story online!

Scan for bonus content

Paul Is Bitten by a Deadly Snake

This story is taken from Acts 28 and
The Acts of the Apostles, chapter 42.

Paul was on his way to Rome to stand trial before Caesar. He had been at sea for many weeks now, but a storm had driven them off course. Now the ship had hit some rocks and was breaking up. There was nothing to do but jump into the ocean to save themselves. Paul had said that God would help them all make it to shore safely, and they did. They all survived the shipwreck. Not one perished.

When everyone had landed on the beach, they discovered that they were on an island called Malta, not far off the coast of Italy. It was late autumn, and the weather was very cold. Everyone was soaking wet and shivering from being in the water, and if that wasn't enough, it now started to rain.

The people living on the island must have seen the ship crash on the rocks, because they came down to the beach to help get a fire going. Wanting to be useful and keep himself warm, Paul helped collect some driftwood. As he was putting some wood on the fire so he could dry out his clothes, a viper bit him. It slithered out of the bundle of wood he was carrying and fastened itself on his hand, but he just shook it off in the fire.

Everyone gasped when they saw the snake hanging on his hand, because they knew it was deadly poisonous. They thought that he must be a very bad criminal to be punished like that by God. "No doubt this man is a murderer," they said among themselves. "Though he has escaped the sea, yet justice does not allow him to live."

However, Paul didn't die as they expected he would. They watched for a while, but were surprised that he didn't swell up or even get dizzy. It was a miracle, and when no harm came to him, they changed their minds and thought he must be a god.

> **Paul had said that God would help them all make it to shore safely, and they did. They all survived the shipwreck.**

On the island lived a man named Publius, a leading citizen of that region. He was very kind to Paul and gave him a place to stay for three days. The father of Publius lay sick with fever and a serious disease called dysentery. Paul felt sorry for him and went to his bedside to pray for him. Then he laid his hands on him and healed him miraculously.

When Paul told the old man that he had been healed by the power of Jesus, he was so grateful to God and praised Him for the miracle. Then everyone on the island

brought to him those who were sick, and Paul ministered to them all, healing them of their diseases.

By now Paul was very famous, and everyone on the island came to honor him before he departed for Rome. It was clear to them that Paul was a special man. Satan had tried to kill him when the ship was wrecked, but God had spared Paul's life and brought him ashore miraculously. Then a deadly poisonous snake had bitten him, but again God saved Paul, and he was able to help the people on the island. With the power of God, Paul healed all of their diseases, and then he told them the story of salvation.

Everyone gasped when they saw the snake hanging on Paul's hand, because they knew it was deadly poisonous.

God had led Paul in all of his travels as a missionary. The apostle had traveled many places to spread the gospel, but it is likely that he would never have come to the island of Malta if God had not let the ship crash on the rocks.

The winter months passed, and finally Paul's group sailed to the port of Syracuse off the coast of Italy. Then they sailed to the port cities of Rhegium and Puteoli, where they stayed with some Christian friends for a week.

By now, friends and relatives in Rome had heard that Paul was coming, and they all went to meet him at the cities of Appii Forum and Three Inns. Paul was so happy to see them, and he thanked God for a safe journey.

When they finally arrived in Rome, the centurion brought all of the prisoners to the captain of the guard. However, Paul was allowed to have his own place with just one soldier to guard him.

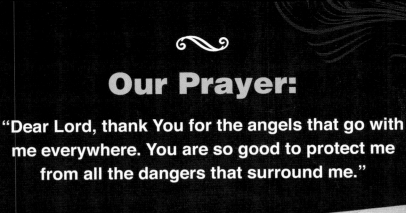

Our Prayer:

"Dear Lord, thank You for the angels that go with me everywhere. You are so good to protect me from all the dangers that surround me."

Hidden Treasure Questions:

✔ What disease did Publius' father have?

✔ Why did the people on the island think Paul was a criminal at first?

Listen to this story online!

Scan for bonus content

Special Armor for God's Special Forces

This story is taken from Ephesians 6, Romans 8,.

While Paul was in prison, he wrote a lot of letters to the churches that he had started. The letters were written to encourage the churches, to tell the believers what God wanted them to do, and to warn them of ways that Satan might try to tempt them.

One of the letters that he wrote was to the church in Ephesus. In this letter, he told the believers that the Christian life is similar to that of a Roman soldier. In Paul's day a soldier needed to wear armor to protect his body and to fight. Special equipment was needed. The belt, sandals, helmet, breastplate, shield, and sword were particularly important. With these things, a soldier could do his job and at the same time protect himself.

In the same way, Christians must wear armor to protect themselves from Satan and the evils in this world. Paul called it the "armor of God."

Paul told the Ephesians, "Be strong in the Lord and in the power of His might. Put on the whole armor of God, that you may be able to stand against the temptations of the devil. For our struggle is not against flesh and blood, but against the rulers, against the authorities, against the powers of this dark world, and against the spiritual forces of evil in the heavenly realms."

Satan and his evil demons would destroy every child of God if they could. But God has promised that if we trust in Him and obey His commandments, He will protect us from the power of Satan.

Christians must wear armor to protect themselves from Satan and the evils in this world. Paul called it the "armor of God."

But we must wear the armor of a Christian. Paul continued, "Therefore, put on the full armor of God, so that when the day of evil comes, you may be able to stand your ground, and after you have done everything, to stand strong. Stand firm with the belt of truth buckled around your waist, with the breastplate of righteousness in place, and with your feet wearing shoes that can take the gospel of peace everywhere. Above all, take up the shield of faith with which you can extinguish all the flaming arrows of the evil one. Also, take the helmet of salvation and the sword of the Spirit, which is the Word of God."

Truth, righteousness, the gospel, faith, salvation, and the Word of God all protect us from Satan and the power of his demons. That is why we must put them on every day, just as a soldier puts on his armor.

Truth, righteousness, the gospel, faith, salvation, and the Word of God all protect us from Satan and the power of his demons.

Jesus' sacrifice on the cross makes all of this possible. That is why we no longer need to worry about whether or not we have eternal life. With this armor on, we are already more than conquerors. We have already been given the tools to protect us from sin and the temptations of Satan.

Jesus loves us more than He loved His place in heaven as the Son of God. That is why nothing can keep us away from our heavenly Father. Paul tells Christians everywhere, "I am persuaded that neither death nor life, nor angels nor principalities nor powers, nor things present nor things to come, nor height nor depth, nor any other created thing, shall be able to separate us from the love of God which is in Christ Jesus our Lord" (Romans 8:38, 39).

That is a pretty amazing promise! It includes everything that God thought might come between Him and us. In the war between good and evil, God knew that we would need all the help we could get, and that is what His armor does for us. With this armor we can be more than conquerors, because we are already victorious in Jesus Christ our Lord.

Our Prayer:

"Dear Father in heaven, help me to always wear the armor that You have provided to protect me from the temptations of this world."

Hidden Treasure Questions:

✔ How many pieces of armor does the Christian need to fight against sin and Satan?

✔ Paul lists 10 things that should not separate us from the love of God. Can you remember what they are?

Listen to this story online!

Scan for bonus content

Paul Helps a Runaway Slave

This story is taken from Philemon and
The Acts of the Apostles, chapter 43.

When Paul was in prison in Rome, many people came to see him. He wasn't chained to a wall like an animal in a cage. Actually, he was given room to move around, with only a guard or two as companions. Today we call that kind of arrangement "house arrest." When Paul was under house arrest, people could come to visit him whenever they wanted.

Timothy was already with him, at least for some of the time that he was in prison. Others soon arrived too. Some came to encourage Paul, some came for advice, and others came simply because they had nowhere else to go. Onesimus was just such a person.

How did he and Paul meet? Onesimus was a runaway slave who had escaped from his master, Philemon, in the city of Colossae and then fled to Rome. In Paul's day, there were many more slaves than Roman citizens in the empire, so runaway slaves were quite common. Onesimus stole money from his master when he escaped, because Paul later offered to pay any debt that Onesimus might have.

Paul told Onesimus that Christians were supposed to be honest and brave. They were supposed to love others.

However, Onesimus had recently become a Christian, and when he did, his life changed forever. He must have heard that there was a great missionary preacher in prison, because that is when he came to see Paul.

Onesimus must have spent some time in prison with Paul, because it wasn't very long before the apostle was treating him like a son. When Paul had heard the young man's story, he advised him to go back to his master in Colossae and become his slave once again.

Does that sound ridiculous? We can be sure that Onesimus must have thought so. Whoever heard of a slave going back to his master if he didn't have to? That is what running away was all about—getting as far away as possible from a slave owner and never going back.

But that was not the way a Christian should do things, Paul told Onesimus. Christians were supposed to be honest and brave. They were supposed to love others. They should be willing to forgive one another's mistakes, even if that someone was a slave owner.

No doubt, Onesimus was afraid to return to his master. Philemon was a Christian now, but since he owned Onesimus, the laws of Rome allowed him to do whatever he wanted with him. He could beat him, sell him to another slave owner, or even kill him. Slaves had no rights and could be bought or sold just as cattle were in a market.

However, Paul prayed and talked with Onesimus about doing the right thing. Then he wrote a personal letter to Philemon and sent Onesimus to hand deliver it himself to his former slave owner.

The letter presented Onesimus to Philemon not as he was before—disloyal and rebellious—but as a brother in Christ.

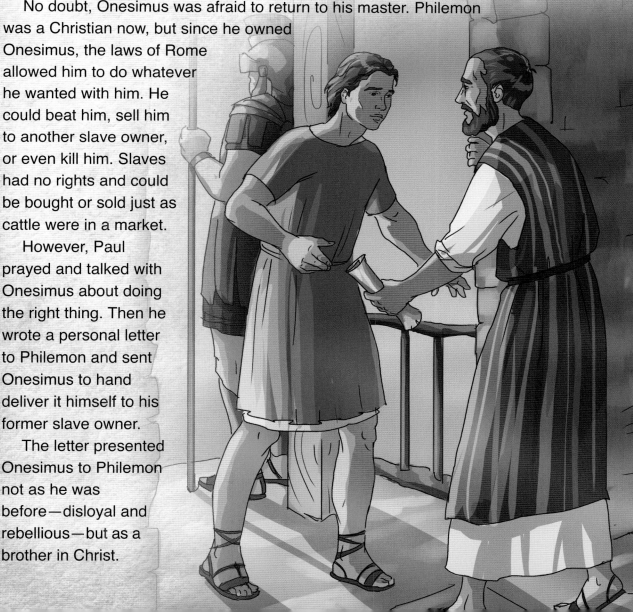

"I appeal to you for my son Onesimus, who became my son while I was chained in prison," said Paul. "Formerly he was useless to you, but now he has become useful both to you and to me. I am sending him—who is my very heart—back to you. I would have preferred to keep him with me. He could take your place in helping me while I am in chains for preaching the gospel.

The letter presented Onesimus to Philemon not as he was before—disloyal and rebellious—but as a brother in Christ.

"But I did not want to do anything without your consent, so that any favor you do would not seem forced, but would be voluntary. Perhaps the reason he was separated from you for a little while was that you might have him back forever—no longer as a slave, but better than a slave—as a dear brother. He is very dear to me, but even dearer to you both as a fellow man and as a brother in the Lord.

"So if you consider me a partner, welcome him as you would welcome me. If he has done you any wrong or owes you anything, charge it to me. I am writing this with my own hand. I will pay it back—not to mention that you owe me your salvation. Confident of your obedience, I write to you knowing that you will do even more than I ask."

The Bible doesn't tell us how this story ended, but we trust it had a happy ending. After all, it was Paul who won both Philemon and Onesimus to Jesus.

"Dear Father in heaven, thank You for paying the pric[e]
for my salvation. I will gladly serve You all my life."

Hidden Treasure Questions:

✔ What was the name of the slave who
ran away from his master, and who
was his master?

✔ What city had the slave run
away from?

Listen to this story online!

Scan for bonus content

Spreading the Gospel From Prison

This story is taken from
The Acts of the Apostles, chapter 44.

Paul had been in prison off and on now for several years. His time in Caesarea and then Rome had not been a time of suffering with him chained to the wall, but he was not free to visit churches either.

Friends came by for visits now and then. Timothy was with him in Rome, and so were Luke and Onesimus, a former slave who became a good friend of Paul while he was in prison. So did several others, including Tychicus and Epaphroditus.

When Christians everywhere heard that Paul was in a prison in Rome, they were shocked and dismayed at first. How could the gospel be spread effectively without Paul to preach it? He was their greatest champion of truth! However, prison life for Paul actually helped the young church grow. Instead of becoming discouraged, the members now realized that they needed to speak even more boldly for Jesus.

But Paul was not idle while in prison. He wrote many letters to the believers to instruct and encourage them. He even sent messengers to take greetings to the Christian churches that he had started. Now his greatest desire was that he might become a witness to the royal family, and for this opportunity he spent much time in prayer.

> **From time to time Paul was called before Nero and his family to witness for his faith.**

Rome was the capital city of the Roman Empire. It was here that Paul was to meet kings, courtiers, and government officers. Nowhere could one find a place less friendly to Christianity than Rome. There were no traces of mercy or compassion in the emperor's heart. In fact, at times he seemed even less than human. Satan was in control of the emperor, Nero, and his closest advisers, and they seemed to be of the same character: fierce, depraved, and wicked.

Some would say that it was useless to bring the gospel story to the pagans of Rome. The most terrible and cruel things were done to Christians in that city. The palace of the Caesars was the stronghold of Satan. How could the message of a crucified and risen Savior make an impression where people lived only for pleasure? How could God's compassion and mercy be shared with people who enjoyed watching gladiators kill each other or Christians being executed on crosses for their faith?

It was true that Christianity was often more appealing to the poor than to the rich. Poor people had little in this world, and the story of salvation offered them hope in the new world to come. The rich and famous, however, were less likely to be interested in the gospel. They had a life of ease and luxury and felt in need of nothing. They might listen to the story of salvation for entertainment if it was presented to them by someone like Paul. He was educated, sophisticated, and witty enough to meet them at their level. Like them, he had been rich at one time and very influential in Jerusalem, so he knew how to reach the hearts of the rich.

Paul's greatest disadvantage was that he had to wait for an invitation, but from time to time he was called before Nero and his family to witness for his faith. Each time he shared the story of his conversion, it made an impression for God upon Paul's listeners. and brought the members of the royal household closer to the cross.

We don't know how Nero himself felt about the salvation story from Paul. However, we do know that there were converts to Christianity in his royal household.

If we are willing to suffer for Jesus as we spread the gospel, we can be a great influence for God. Like Paul, we can sometimes do more for the gospel in a tiny prison cell than we have done in a lifetime of service someplace else. When the servants of Jesus are persecuted, put on trial, or even thrown into prison, they are not forgotten by God. He will give them opportunities, as He did Paul, to speak for Him, and to let the light of the gospel shine so that others can see the way to Jesus.

> **Like Paul, we can sometimes do more for the gospel in a tiny prison cell than we have done in a lifetime of service someplace else.**

It is said that Paul did more to spread the story of salvation to the world than anyone before or after him. Whether he was preaching to a packed synagogue on the Sabbath day or teaching a new convert one-on-one, Paul let the Holy Spirit shine through him.

That is what we must do for Jesus. Today we are free and able to speak to whomever we wish, wherever we wish. However, someday soon, we may be locked up in a prison cell. When that time comes, it may be that we will be even better witnesses for Jesus.

Our Prayer:

"Dear Jesus, I know that someday You may ask me to witness for You from a prison cell. Help me to be faithful now so that I can be faithful then."

Hidden Treasure Questions:

✔ What was the capital city of the Roman Empire?

✔ What was the name of the emperor in Rome when Paul was put into prison?

Listen to this story online!

Scan for bonus content

I Have Fought the Good Fight

This story is taken from
The Acts of the Apostles, chapters 46-50.

Paul stayed in the Roman prison for many months, and his friends were given freedom to come and go as they pleased. However, the Jews were still anxious to have Paul convicted, and they hoped to get some help from Nero's second wife, who was also a Jew. Things did not look good for Paul now, and he realized that he could expect very little mercy from Emperor Nero.

Nero was becoming more evil as the years passed. During the first year of his reign, he had poisoned his stepbrother, who was the rightful heir to the throne. Then he murdered his mother and his first wife. Even those who served in his court were afraid of what he might do next. Still, they gave him their allegiance. He was the emperor of the whole civilized world, and they worshipped him as if he was a god.

Then strangely enough, after examining Paul's case, Nero found no guilt in him and set him free. It was all a great mystery, something that no one would have ever expected, but Paul knew that God had arranged everything.

Now Paul could travel again, so he went throughout Asia Minor to visit all his churches.

During the next year, however, times became very difficult for the Christians in Rome. The number of Christians had increased, and Nero was furious because members of his own household had become Christians. Everyone knew that he hated the Christians, and before long he found a way to get even with them.

Strangely enough, after examining Paul's case, Nero found no guilt in him and set him free. Paul knew that God had arranged everything.

At this time a terrible fire started in Rome, and nearly half the city was destroyed. Many were suspicious that Nero himself had started the fire, and they were very angry about it. The emperor realized that his life was in danger over the matter, so he turned the blame on the Christians. In the months that followed, thousands of Christian men, women, and children were executed in the cruelest ways.

Paul had escaped Rome just in time, but the troublesome Jews were still after him. They accused him of setting fire to Rome, and before long he was arrested on those charges. They knew that Paul was not capable of doing such a thing, but they hated him so much that they didn't care.

The final years of mercy for the Jews, as a race of people, were fast closing.

They had crucified the Son of God and killed Christians such as Stephen and James. Now they were persecuting God's people everywhere, including Paul, the greatest missionary of the church. In less than a decade, a major revolt by the Jews in Judea would bring the wrath of Rome upon Jerusalem. Unfortunately, God would not be able to save them. Like King Saul, they had destroyed every possible channel by which God could reach them.

The troublesome Jews were still after him. They accused him of setting fire to Rome.

Before long Paul was arrested and brought back to Rome, and this time he didn't escape condemnation. Many wanted to go to prison with him and share his fate, but he wouldn't let them endanger their lives. Thousands in Rome had already been martyred for their faith, and many more had left the city.

Paul was put into a gloomy prison cell with just a few of his friends to encourage him. Some, such as Hermogenes and Demas, left him because they were afraid. Others, such as Titus and Tychicus, were sent to work in the churches that Paul had started. Only Luke stayed with Paul, and what a blessing he was!

Another trial was set for the aging apostle, and again, he had a chance to defend himself. Everyone was afraid of Nero, but not Paul. He had received visits from Jesus and angels, and nothing could shake his faith in the promises of God. With the power of the Holy Spirit, Paul spoke of Jesus' death and resurrection. He talked of coming judgments against those who persecuted the children of God. Nero trembled at Paul's words and realized that he must answer to God someday for the way that he treated people.

However, it was for only a moment that Nero felt the call of God. He was afraid to sentence Paul to death, but he didn't set him free, either. When he sent Paul back to his prison cell, his last chance to hear the gospel was gone.

Paul spent the remaining days of his life praying for his churches and writing to his friend Timothy, who was by now a pastor in the city of Ephesus. In his last letter to Timothy, he wrote, "I have fought the good fight, I have finished the race, I have kept the faith. Finally, there is laid up for me the crown of righteousness, which the Lord, the righteous Judge, will give to me on that Day, and not to me only but also to all who have loved His appearing" (2 Timothy 4:7, 8).

What a testimony for Paul, who had given his life for the gospel. What a blessing it was for Timothy to receive such words of encouragement in the last letter that Paul would ever write for the church.

Not long after this, Nero made his decision to have Paul executed. The wicked emperor had been kind to Paul in the previous trial, but his anger toward Christians had grown only stronger now. He seemed unable to stop his own family from accepting Christianity, and for this, he decided that Paul must pay with his life.

Paul was taken under guard to the place of execution, and few were allowed to be present and watch. His enemies were afraid that if people were allowed to witness the execution, they might become Christians too. However, because he was a Roman citizen he could not be tortured, and so he was sentenced to be beheaded.

The hardened soldiers probably thought that this would be similar to every other execution, but they were wrong. Paul was a servant of the living God. He had been called out of darkness into God's marvelous light, and he was not willing that these soldiers should perish. His dying words were for the men who executed him.

Nero made his decision to have Paul executed. The wicked emperor's anger toward Christians had grown.

When he died, some at the execution gave their lives to Jesus because of Paul's stand for God. His forgiving spirit and faith in Jesus amazed them such as no one had ever done. The look of peace and light on his face was like that of an angel, and it made them want what he had.

Nero, on the other hand, never had a day of peace after he sentenced Paul to his death. Not long after this, messengers came running to the palace to tell Nero that General Galba was coming to Rome to take the throne by force. Nero had no one to protect him, and he certainly did not have a Savior on whom he could call.

He tried to end his own life, but didn't have the courage. Alone and afraid, he fled the city to hide, but was followed. As he saw the enemy horsemen approaching, he finally managed to take his own life and died at the young age of 30. So ended the life of the man who dared to take the life of Paul, Christianity's greatest champion.

Our Prayer:

"Dear Jesus, I want to be as brave as Paul was and never be afraid to speak for You."

Hidden Treasure Questions:

✔ What happened when Emperor Nero examined Paul?

✔ To whom did Paul write his last letter?

Listen to this story online!

Scan for bonus content

Peter Is
Faithful to the End

This story is taken from
The Acts of the Apostles, chapters 51 and 52.

Peter was one of the most unusual people in the Bible. He was tough, but he had the heart of a child. He made a living on the lake fishing, and that's how Jesus had found him. There was great potential in this man, and Jesus recognized it. "Follow Me, and I will make you become a fisher of men," He had said. Immediately, Peter left his nets and followed the Man from Nazareth.

But Peter was impatient and often spoke before he really thought about what he was saying. Sometimes he was more of a bodyguard for Jesus than a childlike student at the Teacher's feet. When mothers brought their children to see Jesus, Peter turned them away rudely. When officers from the temple asked Peter if Jesus usually paid the temple tax, he said "Yes," forgetting that Jesus was a rabbi and was therefore not required to pay such taxes.

When Jesus asked the disciples, "Who do you say that I am?" Peter was the first to say that Jesus was the Christ, the Son of the living God. He may have been impulsive and quick to speak, but he was genuine.

Jesus knew that Peter was sincere, but He also knew that Peter was weak in some areas. Peter promised that he would be faithful to death, but on the night before Jesus was crucified, he swore that he had never even met "the Man." By the time the rooster crowed a second time, Peter had denied the Lord three times, just as Jesus had predicted he would.

When Peter saw Jesus looking at him sadly from across the courtyard of the high priest, it broke his heart. In shame, he ran from the palace, horrified at what he had done.

But Jesus wasn't finished teaching Peter a lesson. A few weeks after His resurrection, He asked Peter a question while walking on the beach with him. "Do you love Me?" Jesus asked.

"Yes, Lord," was all Peter could say. "You know that I love You!"

Twice more Jesus asked the same question of Peter. Twice more the disciple confessed with tears that he did love Jesus. "Yes, Lord! You know all things! You know that I love You!"

Then Jesus did something very unusual. He opened the doors of the future to give Peter a glimpse of what was in store for him. The disciple was going to die on a cruel cross, just as Jesus Himself had suffered.

But strangely enough, Peter didn't seem to be too worried. He had walked and talked with the Son of God. By God's grace he would remain faithful no matter what the cost, even if it should be death!

What a contrast to the life of Peter before he had been converted. His experience on the night of Jesus' trial brought him much grief, but he prayed that God might forgive him.

Jesus asked Peter a question while walking on the beach with him. "Do you love Me?" Jesus asked.

And God made him into a new man. After he repented and received the Holy Spirit on the Day of Pentecost, he went on to become a great leader of the early church. Thousands were baptized in a day because of his preaching. People were healed by him, and demons were cast out. Some were even raised from the dead, all because he had surrendered his life to Jesus.

But Satan wasn't happy with what Peter was doing for Jesus and the church. He possessed evil men to treat Peter very badly. He was beaten and put in prison many times, and at least twice angels freed him from prison bars.

Peter became a pastor of the gospel to both Jews and Gentiles. He wrote letters to the early Christians to encourage them. Eventually those letters became books in the Bible. Today we call them First Peter and Second Peter.

Peter gave his life for the One whom he had denied so many years before. One day soon Jesus will come, and He will raise Peter to life.

After many years of success as an evangelist, he was finally captured and sent to Rome during the reign of Emperor Nero. He was condemned for his faith in Jesus and sentenced to die by crucifixion. However, he remembered with shame the way that he had treated Jesus the night before His death and made one last request. He asked to be crucified upside down, because he didn't feel worthy to die the same way that Jesus had died.

So it was that Peter gave his life for the One whom he had denied so many years before. One day soon Jesus will come, and He will raise Peter to life. You and I will get to see the two of them together again. What a meeting that will be!

Our Prayer:

"Dear God, help me to be as faithful as Peter was so that I can share the gospel everywhere."

Hidden Treasure Questions:

✔ What are some things that Peter did to make the early Christian church strong in Jesus?

✔ How did Peter die?

Listen to this story online!

Scan for bonus content

John Is Boiled in Oil

This story is taken from Revelation 1 and
The Acts of the Apostles, chapters 53-56.

John the Beloved was quite young when he first met Jesus. He was born in Galilee and was a fisherman by trade. He became interested in Jesus as the Messiah when he heard John the Baptist preaching about "the Lamb of God who takes away the sin of the world." When he left his fishing boats to follow Jesus, he became the most faithful of disciples. Soon he was known as Jesus' closest companion and was rarely absent from His side.

For more than three years, he walked the roads of Galilee and Judea witnessing Jesus' rise to fame. He heard Jesus' message of peace, hope, and love, and was surprised at the authority with which the Savior preached. He saw the Master perform amazing miracles as He healed the lame, blind, and deaf. He watched Jesus cast out demons and cleanse lepers. Surely, this Man from Galilee was indeed the Son of God!

John was one of the few to witness Jesus' struggle with demons in the Garden of Gethsemane. He was stunned as he watched the trial of Jesus and His crucifixion on Golgotha. After Jesus' resurrection and ascension to heaven, John remained in Jerusalem for more than 10 years, where he stood for truth and helped evangelize Jerusalem.

Throughout his lifetime, John endured much for the sake of the gospel. As a Christian in the early church, he suffered cruel beatings and imprisonment. He even escaped from prison with the help of angels. When persecution from Herod Agrippa made it impossible to preach the gospel in Judea any longer, he fled with Peter to Samaria. Then he traveled to Asia Minor, where he helped build up the church.

According to church historians, he had witnessed the destruction of Jerusalem. He was later arrested and brought to Rome during the reign of the Emperor Domitian. The cruel emperor ordered that John be executed by being thrown into a vat of boiling oil, but miraculously the faithful disciple was preserved unharmed.

The beloved disciple was then banished to the Isle of Patmos to keep him from spreading the gospel. But John's work for God wasn't finished yet. While on the Greek island, he received visions to instruct him and many visits from angels to encourage him to be faithful.

Even Jesus Himself visited John to give him special messages for the church. In the first chapter of Revelation, John describes what Jesus looked like. "His head and hair were white like wool, as white as snow, and His eyes like a flame of fire," said John. "His feet were like fine brass, as if refined in a furnace, and His voice as the sound of many waters. His countenance was like the sun shining in its strength." And when John saw Him, he fell on his face, but Jesus touched him and said, "Do not be afraid; I am the First and the Last. I am He who lives, and was dead, and behold, I am alive forevermore."

He watched Jesus cast out demons and cleanse lepers. Surely, this Man from Galilee was indeed the Son of God!

John wrote in the book of Revelation about all the things that he saw in vision while he was on the Isle of Patmos. Revelation tells about the war between good and evil and unveils the mysteries of the future. Some of the things that John wrote about include the seven churches, the dragon and the woman, the mark of the beast, the 144,000, the three angels' messages, the seven last plagues, Jesus' second coming, the millennium, and a new heaven and earth.

John wrote in the book of Revelation about all the things that he saw in vision while he was on the Isle of Patmos.

About A.D. 96, when a new emperor came to the throne in Rome, John was released from prison and allowed to go to the city of Ephesus, where he became a pillar of the church. His favorite topic was always about the love that Christian brothers and sisters should have for one another. "My little children, let us not love in word or in tongue, but in deed and in truth" (1 John 3:18).

John lived to a ripe old age in Ephesus, Asia Minor, where it is said that he died and was buried about A.D. 100. As Jesus predicted, John was the only one of the original 12 disciples to die a natural death.

This most beloved of the apostles left behind five books that can be found in the New Testament: the Gospel of John, the three letters to the early church, which are 1 John, 2 John, and 3 John, and the book of Revelation. One day soon Jesus will come again and reward John the Beloved for his faithful years of service. What a day that will be!

Our Prayer:

"Dear Father in heaven, help me to be as true to You as John."

Hidden Treasure Questions:

✔ On which island was John imprisoned to keep him from preaching the gospel?

✔ What are some of the things that he wrote about in the book of Revelation?

Listen to this story online!

Scan for bonus content

Seven Messages From Seven Churches

This story is taken from Revelation 2 and 3.

Near the end of his life, John received many messages from God. These messages can be found in the book of Revelation, which is the last book in the Bible. Revelation is a collection of prophecies about things such as saints, angels, dragons, and plagues.

John was given a message from Jesus about seven churches that were located in Asia Minor in what is now called the country of Turkey. Each church was unique in the good things that it was doing for God and the kind of troubles it was facing. John's message was also prophetic, because the seven churches represent seven periods of church history since the time of Jesus. These symbolic churches stretch all the way from the first church that the disciples started in Jerusalem to the last church of our day, just before Jesus comes again.

> These symbolic churches stretch all the way from the first church that the disciples started in Jerusalem to the last church of our day, just before Jesus comes again.

This prophecy was included in the book of Revelation so that you and I can see how God has led His church in the past. It was also written so that we will know what to expect from His world church as we near the end of time.

The first church was called Ephesus, named for the Christian church in the city of Ephesus. This church represented the earliest period in Christian history when the church was just starting out and growing so fast. Jesus said that He was pleased with this church because they were hard workers, had endured hardships, and would not give up their desire to spread the gospel. Also, they would not allow evil people to spoil the church. However, there were a few things that Jesus was not happy about with this church. The people in the Ephesus church had given up their first love. Now Jesus was challenging them to repent of their sins and become faithful disciples of Him, just as they had been at the start. Jesus promised, "To the one who is victorious, I will give the right to eat from the tree of life, which is in the paradise of God."

ASIA

THE SEVEN CHURCHES OF REVELATION

ÆGEAN SEA

MEDITERRANEAN SEA

GALATIA

°Pergamun

°Thyatira

°Sardis

°Philadelphia

°Smyrna

°Ephesus

°Laodicea

The church was a pure church, patient in service and love.

The second church was in Smyrna, and was the church of suffering. It is thought that this church represented the time of great persecution during the second and third centuries A.D.

During this time the Christians had many trials and troubles. They were poor in the things of this world, but rich in faith. Jesus told the people of this church, "Do not be afraid of what you are about to suffer. I tell you, the devil will put some of you into prison to test you, and you will suffer persecution for 10 days. Be faithful, even to the point of death, and I will give you a victor's crown, so that you will not be hurt at all by the second death."

The third church was called Pergamos. This church wanted to remain true to God, but ended up being the church of compromise. In other words, they were willing to give up their faith if they could have peace instead of trials. Jesus told these Christians, "To the one who is victorious, I will give some of the hidden manna. I will also give that person a white stone with a new name written on it, known only to the one who receives it." This period in church history lasted for more than two centuries.

The fourth church was named Thyatira and was guilty of apostasy down through the Dark Ages of medieval times. Some in the church at that time were loving and faithful to serve God with perseverance. Jesus told this church, "Hold on to what you have until I come." However, for the most part, the church of this period rebelled against God and did many wicked things. Jesus compared this church to Jezebel, who had tempted Israel to be unfaithful to God. He gave the church time to repent of its sins, but it would not.

The fifth church was called Sardis. God saw that it would reform from its evil ways. It lasted for about two centuries following the Protestant Reformation in Europe. Unfortunately, it was a church that did not live by faith, but by works. God warned the people of this church to wake up and repent, but He also encouraged the ones who were being faithful. "They shall walk with Me, dressed in white, for they are worthy," Jesus said. "I will never blot out the name of these persons from the Book of Life, but will present their names before My Father and before His angels."

Philadelphia was the name of the sixth church. This was a time of revival in the church. It was a time when the gospel was being spread to all the world. This time period ran for about 50 years and lasted until about the mid-1800s. The church was a pure church, patient in service and love. Jesus told them, "I am coming soon. Hold on to what you have, that no one may take your crown. The one who is victorious, I will make a pillar in the temple of My God."

The final church was called Laodicea. Jesus saw this church as the last-day church. It was neither cold nor hot spiritually. They would be rich in the things of this world and think they needed nothing. Unfortunately, they wouldn't realize that they were wretched, pitiful, poor, blind, and naked. Jesus told the people in this church, "I counsel you to buy from Me gold refined in the fire, that you may be rich. I will give you white clothes to wear so that you can cover your shameful nakedness, and salve to put on your eyes so that you can see." To those who are victorious, Jesus says, "I will give the right to sit with Me on My throne."

Jesus loves His church, but knows that He must sometimes rebuke and discipline it. He begs His church to listen to His voice. "I stand at the door and knock. If anyone hears My voice and opens the door, I will come in to him and dine with him, and he with Me." He promises wonderful things to those who overcome the temptations of Satan. "To the one who is victorious, I will give the right to sit with Me on My throne, just as I was victorious and sat down with My Father on His throne."

To those who are victorious, Jesus says, "I will give the right to sit with Me on My throne."

God has always had a church to represent Him down through history. Some churches were more faithful than others, but all were called to spread the gospel and to stand for Him against the forces of evil.

Our Prayer:

"Dear Father in heaven, I pray that I can help the people in my church prepare for Jesus' soon coming."

Hidden Treasure Questions:

✔ How many churches did John write about in Revelation, and what were their names?

✔ What kind of people are found in the church of our day?

Listen to this story online!

Scan for bonus content

A Woman and a Child Hunted by a Dragon

This story is taken from Revelation 12.

While John was imprisoned on the Isle of Patmos, he received visions from God about the war between good and evil. This war had been raging for thousands of years, since the beginning of the world. It was clear that this war was not an imaginary one.

Several visions given to John made the struggle with evil seem even more real. In one vision, he saw the very first battle between good and evil in heaven. He wrote about it: "Michael and His angels fought with the dragon; and the dragon and his angels fought, but they did not prevail, nor was a place found for them in heaven any longer. So the great dragon was cast out, that serpent of old, called the Devil and Satan, who deceives the whole world; he was cast to the earth, and his angels were cast out with him" (Revelation 12:7-9).

Like a roaring lion, Satan now attacked the church to destroy it through persecution.

John saw that Satan would not go away easily. He tempted Adam and Eve to become evil like him, and they fell into sin. From that day forward evil became the master of this world.

Then John saw "a woman clothed with the sun, with the moon under her feet, and on her head a garland of 12 stars. Then being with child, she cried out in labor and in pain to give birth" (Revelation 12:1, 2). The dragon called the Devil and Satan knew that he had lost his place in heaven and was very angry with God's people. Therefore, "he stood before the woman who was ready to give birth, to devour her Child as soon as it was born" (verse 4).

However, when she gave birth to the Baby, the little Child grew up to fulfill the prophecy by dying on the cross to crush the serpent's head (Genesis 3:15). The woman represented God's church, and the Child was Jesus.

Satan knew that his doom was sure, because Jesus had died to save the world from sin. Like a roaring lion, Satan now attacked the church to destroy it through persecution.

But God had a plan to deliver the church. She was "given two wings of a great eagle, that she might fly into the wilderness to her place, where she is nourished for a time and times and half a time, from the presence of the serpent" (Revelation 12:14). John also refers to this space of time as 1,260 days, which are understood to be prophetic years.

During the Dark Ages of medieval history, there were many Christians who chose to be true to God and the Bible. Their faith in God's promises was strong, and they decided to obey Him no matter what the cost. Many fled away into the wilderness areas of Europe to escape persecution. God in His mercy gave them a refuge, but Satan and his evil angels were not content with this.

History tells us that the Church of Rome chased Christians into the mountains to catch them and force them to obey the church instead of God. John saw this in one of his visions when "the serpent spewed water out of his mouth like a flood after the woman, that he might cause her to be carried away by the flood" (Revelation 12:15).

But again, God had a plan to save His people. "The earth helped the woman,

Then John saw "a woman clothed with the sun, with the moon under her feet, and on her head a garland of 12 stars."

and the earth opened its mouth and swallowed up the flood which the dragon had spewed out of his mouth" (Revelation 12:16). At this time in history, God provided a way for great migrations of people to make the trip across the Atlantic Ocean to find religious freedom in the Americas.

"And the dragon was enraged with the woman, and he went to make war with the rest of her offspring, who keep the commandments of God and have the testimony of Jesus Christ" (Revelation 12:17). During the last few hundred years, Satan has been persecuting Christians, especially those who want to keep all of God's commandments and are willing to share their faith in spreading the gospel.

As world history draws to a close, Satan will increase his efforts to destroy God's people. He is as angry as a lion seeking its prey, because he knows that his time is short. However, God's people will overcome the temptations of Satan. How will they do that? Revelation 12 tells us that they "overcame him by the blood of the Lamb and by the word of their testimony, and they did not love their lives to the death" (verse 11). In other words, they trusted that Jesus will save them from this wicked old world, even if they must die for Him while they spread the gospel.

"Dear Jesus, thank You for helping me overcome the temptations of Satan, the dragon. Help me to be faithful in following you."

Hidden Treasure Questions:

✔ Whom do the dragon, the child, and the woman represent in prophecy?

✔ How did the woman escape the persecutions of the dragon?

Listen to this story online!

Scan for bonus content

John Receives a Heavenly Vision

This story is taken from Revelation 4 and Daniel 7.

While John was a prisoner on the Isle of Patmos, he had many visions and dreams about things to come. One of his most impressive visions was a scene of heaven's throne room as recorded in the book of Revelation. John wrote what he saw so that you and I might catch a glimpse of what heaven's throne room looks like. Unfortunately, human words can only say so much.

"I looked, and there was a door standing open in heaven," said John. "And the first voice which I heard was like a trumpet speaking with me, saying, 'Come up here, and I will show you things which must take place after this.' At once I was in the Spirit, and there before me was a throne in heaven with Someone sitting on it. And the One who sat there had the appearance of jasper and ruby. There was a rainbow that shone like an emerald around the throne.

"Surrounding the throne were 24 other thrones, and seated on them were 24 elders. They were dressed in white and had crowns of gold on their heads. From the throne came flashes of lightning, rumblings, and peals of thunder. In front of the throne, seven lamps were blazing. These are the seven spirits of God. Also in front of the throne there was what looked like a sea of glass, clear as crystal."

Then John described mysterious creatures in heaven's throne room, which sound very strange indeed to us as humans: "In the center, around the throne, were four living creatures, and they were covered with eyes in front and in back. The first living creature was like a lion, the second was like a calf, the third had a face like a man, and the fourth was like a flying eagle. Each of the four living creatures had six wings and were covered with eyes all around, even under its wings."

But the most important part of this description is what the creatures were doing. John says, "Day and night they never stop saying, 'Holy, holy, holy, is the Lord God Almighty, who was, and is, and is to come!'"

"Surrounding the throne were 24 other thrones, and seated on them were 24 elders. They were dressed in white and had crowns."

Whenever these living creatures give glory to God, showering Him with honor and thanking Him who sits on the throne, the 24 elders join them. They all fall down before the Creator, who sits on heaven's throne, and worship Him who lives for ever and ever.

But even this is not enough. Every ounce of energy that these creatures have is given in loving worship as they lay their crowns before the throne. "You are worthy, O Lord, to receive glory and honor and power; for You created all things, and by Your will they exist and were created" (Revelation 4:11).

John's words are a wonderful description of what he saw. We should be very grateful that God gave him a picture for us to read. That way we can be reverent when we speak His name and excited about what it will be like to see God someday.

But John is not the only one in the Bible who saw God on His throne. Daniel was also privileged to see such scenes in visions that God gave him. He says, "I watched till thrones were put in place, and the Ancient of Days was seated; His garment was white as snow, and the hair of His head was like pure wool. His throne was a fiery flame, its wheels a burning fire. A fiery stream issued and came forth from before Him. A thousand thousands ministered to Him; ten thousand times ten thousand stood before Him" (Daniel 7:9, 10).

Then Daniel said that he saw the Son of Man, who was Jesus, "coming with the clouds of heaven" and joining the Father in the throne room. He approached the Ancient of Days, and was led into His presence. He was given authority, glory, and sovereign power, and all nations and peoples of every language worshipped Him. Daniel wrote: "His dominion is an everlasting dominion, which shall not pass away, and His kingdom the one which shall not be destroyed" (Daniel 7:14).

Someday we will go to heaven, and there we will see heaven's throne room as these two men saw it so long ago. The angels, 24 elders, and four living creatures see God every day. But even so, they are awed by the brilliance of His glory, the warmth of His wonderful presence, and the great love that He has for all His creation.

As sons and daughters of King Jesus, we can only say, "Come, Lord Jesus, and take us home to heaven! We can hardly wait!"

Day and night they never stop saying, "Holy, holy, holy, is the Lord God Almighty, who was, and is, and is to come!"

Our Prayer:

"Dear Father in heaven, I cannot imagine what it will be like to worship You in heaven's throne room. Help me practice being reverent now in church every week."

Hidden Treasure Questions:

✔ What three precious gems does John use to describe God's heavenly throne?

✔ How many elders and living creatures worship God continually in His throne room?

Listen to this story online!

Scan for bonus content

God Leads His Church to Success

This story is taken from
The Acts of the Apostles, chapter 58.

Years have come and gone since Jesus went back to heaven. When Jesus gave His church power on the Day of Pentecost to spread the gospel to the world, they fulfilled His commission and did just that. Men such as Peter, John, and Paul went everywhere sharing the story of salvation.

Most of the people who won souls for the kingdom of God were not educated. They just loved God and wanted to be part of the last great message to the world. They wanted people to see that Satan had already lost the war between good and evil.

This is very important because God uses everybody. Jesus has a very important work for each one of us to do. Whether we are rich or poor, He still wants our help in witnessing to others. If we are in college or haven't even started school yet, we can each be a witness for Christ.

Remember Jesus took unlearned fishermen and farmers and made them into great disciples. He can and will do the same thing for you and me.

As Jesus' disciples went everywhere sharing the gospel, both Jews and Gentiles heard the Word of God. The message became very popular, and people welcomed the hope of a new world to come. Within a few short decades the gospel went to the civilized world of ancient Rome, and even into Asia, Africa, and Europe.

Christians were dragged before kings and governments to testify for their faith. They were betrayed by friends and family.

This made Satan very upset. When Christ went back to heaven after His resurrection Satan had to be very happy. He must have thought that with Christ gone from this earth it will be a lot easier to keep the people from believing in God. But to his surprise that is not what happened at all. Instead they were more excited in preaching the gospel than when Christ was here on the earth with them.

Satan realized that he must stop the Christians, or his kingdom of darkness would end. Soon the whole world would know the story of salvation, and then Jesus would come. So he set out to persecute the church in terrible ways. Christians were dragged before kings and governments to testify for their faith. They were betrayed by friends and family. They were beaten and tortured, and many died for their testimony. During the days of the caesars they were taken to the amphitheaters of Rome to provide entertainment on holidays. Thousands were crucified; others were thrown in with wild animals and torn apart. Many Christians were burned alive because they would not give up their faith in God.

But the blood of the martyrs became the seed of the church, which means that every time someone died for their belief many others made the decision to witness for Christ in their place. The number of Christians continued to grow even though Satan caused many to die. Finally Satan realized that his strategy to destroy Christianity wasn't working, so he came up with a new plan to stop the good news from spreading further.

He convinced government leaders such as the emperor Constantine to accept Christianity and then introduce false ideas into the church to corrupt it. These leaders said that they wanted everyone to get along and worship together so that there would be peace on earth. Many Christians were suspicious, but they were tired of persecution, so they listened to the leaders.

They were right to be afraid. Before long deceptions were creeping into the church, such as the Sabbath being changed to Sunday. People were also taught that praying to images of the saints was a good thing. Soon everyone was looking to church leaders for instruction instead of reading their Bibles for themselves.

Little by little the church weakened as it accepted these new ideas, and it became corrupt. The bishop of Rome became the head of the church as a pope, and then the church lost its identity. The Bible was no longer used to spread the gospel as the church developed its own rules and traditions.

A great time of spiritual darkness descended on the world as ignorance and superstition grew. The common people couldn't afford an education, so most of them could not read. Soon there were almost no more Bibles, and it looked as if Satan had finally won the war between good and evil.

But God still had His chosen ones who stood for Him. Many such as Wycliffe and Luther translated the Bible for people to read, and a great time of spiritual awakening came during the Protestant Reformation. Satan tortured and killed many faithful champions to stop the growth of the Reformation, but the light of truth prevailed.

During the 1700s and 1800s, a great missionary movement began. The gospel now went with great power to every nation, tongue, and people on earth. The message of Jesus' soon coming was proclaimed such as it had not been preached since the days of the early church. People preached the message far and wide, and the church received a powerful outpouring of the Holy Spirit to help it grow.

Why is this story so important? It is because Satan is still using the same strategy and tricks on us today. When times were so dangerous and tough for the Christians those who were faithful were ready for anything. They were even willing to die for their faith if necessary.

But as we just read, when things got much easier their guard was let down and Satan was able to trick them much easier. We have been told in God's Word that there will come a time when Satan will influence men with authority to make life miserable for us. We will have to rely on our faith in Jesus more than ever to make it through just like the disciples did.

Little by little the church weakened as it accepted these new ideas, and it became corrupt.

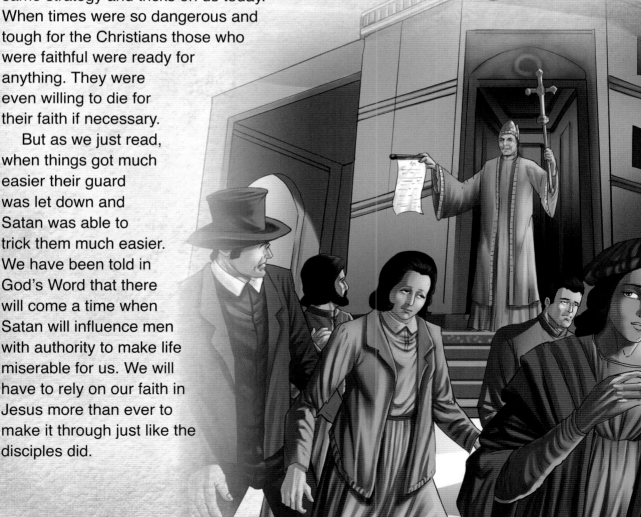

Don't be fooled into thinking that just because we are not being persecuted that Satan isn't working on us. Satan is working harder than ever. So we have to be ready even when things seem to be going good.

People preached the message, and the church received a powerful outpouring of the Holy Spirit.

Today we eagerly await the soon coming of Jesus, as all Christians have down through the ages. But the fulfillment of Jesus' promise is almost complete. He said, "And this gospel of the kingdom will be preached in all the world as a witness to all the nations, and then the end will come" (Matthew 24:14).

We are almost there. The gospel is now being preached in every country on earth. Entire Bibles are being printed in more than 530 languages. Radio, television, and satellites are proclaiming the gospel to the world, and people are going door-to-door to tell the good news.

The great controversy between Christ and Satan is nearly finished now, and when it is, the church will have triumphed over evil. Then Jesus will come and take His people home. Are you ready for that day to come?

"Dear Heavenly Father, help me to do my part to spread the good news of God's love for His church."

Hidden Treasure Questions:

✔ How did Satan try to stop the early church from spreading the gospel?

✔ In how many languages has the Bible been published?

Listen to this story online!

Scan for bonus content

I
THOU SHALT HAVE
NO OTHER GODS
BEFORE ME

II
THOU SHALT NOT
MAKE UNTO THEE
ANY GRAVEN IMAGE

III
THOU SHALT NOT
TAKE THE NAME OF
THE LORD THY GOD
IN VAIN

IV
REMEMBER THE
SABBATH DAY TO
KEEP IT HOLY

V
HONOR THY FATHER
AND THY MOTHER

VI
THOU SHALT
NOT KILL

VII
THOU SHALT NOT
COMMIT ADULTERY

VIII
THOU SHALT
NOT STEAL

IX
THOU SHALT NOT
BEAR FALSE
WITNESS AGAINST
THY NEIGHBOR

X
THOU SHALT
NOT COVET

TO THE
UNKNOWN
GOD